The Combat Sports Strength and Conditioning Manual

— Minimalist Training for Maximum Results —

Will Morrill

The Combat Sports Strength and Conditioning Manual
© 2018 Will Morrill. All rights reserved.

For more information visit **combatsportsmanual.com**
Password for extra content: FIGHTSTRENGTH

Book Cover Design: Marissa Torre
Cover Photo: Ronin Advertising
Pictured on Cover: Will Morrill and "Iron City" Mike Wilkins
Editors: Ben Major and Marissa Torre
Neck Strength Photos: Quinn Jordan

ISBN: 9781792616365

The information in this book is for educational purposes only and is not intended as a substitute for individual health and fitness advice. You should be in good physical condition before beginning this or any other exercise system. The author is not a licensed practitioner, physician or medical professional and offers no medical treatments, diagnoses, suggestions or counseling. The information presented herein has not been evaluated by the U.S. Food and Drug Administration, and is not intended to diagnose, treat, cure or prevent any disease. Full medical clearance from a licensed physician should be obtained before beginning or modifying any diet, exercise or combat sports program, and physicians should be informed of all nutritional changes. The author claims no responsibility to any person or entity for any liability, injury, loss or damage caused or alleged to be caused directly or indirectly as a result of the use, application or interpretation of the information presented herein.

Acknowledgements

I would like to thank:

- Warren Stout and Mike Wilkins for elevating my understanding of MMA and giving me all of the opportunities that you have.

- Bob Meese for showing me the intricacies of boxing in MMA.

- All the MMA, Muay Thai fighters, and team members at Stout Training Pittsburgh for the hard work and dedication you have put into the fight game.

- My college coaches David Vacco, Os Omo-Osagie, and the late Jack Rorabaugh for teaching me how to box.

- My Tang Soo Do instructor DeWayne Adams for showing me where traditional martial arts overlap with fighting and how they differ, as well as for introducing me to lifting weights.

- John Swisher from Ronin Advertising for sending me all the great photos.

- My parents, family and friends for putting up with all this fighting nonsense for so many years.

- Marissa for designing the cover, website, and supporting me through the whole writing process.

Table of Contents

— Chapter 1 — **Introduction** — - 7 -

— Chapter 2 — **Programming a Week and Cycle** — - 15 -

— Chapter 3 — **Exercise Selection** — - 19 -

— Chapter 4 — **Loading Schemes** — - 35 -

— Chapter 5 — **Strength Benchmarks** — - 51 -

— Chapter 6 — **Peaking** — - 55 -

— Chapter 7 — **Conditioning** — - 61 -

— Chapter 8 — **Cutting Weight** — - 67 -

— Chapter 9 — **Nutrition** — - 77 -

— Chapter 10 — **Neck Strength** — - 87 -

— Chapter 11 — **Tracking Sheets** — - 95 -

— Chapter 12 — **Application to Non-MMA Combat Sports** — - 101 -

— Chapter 13 — **Mental Training** — - 105 -

— Chapter 14 — **Movement Tables** — - 111 -

— Chapter 15 — **References** — - 121 -

— Chapter 1 —

Introduction

The mission of this manual is to provide quality information about strength training to the coaches and athletes who dedicate their lives to combat sports. Combat sports have often sat on the back burner of society in the United States, while arguably more violent sports such as football and hockey have flourished. Many factors separate combat sports from the major big money sports, and one small way to help close the gap and elevate the standing of combat sports is to bring the high level strength and conditioning training from other sports over and apply it intelligently. At the college and sometimes even the high-school level, team sports have designated strength and conditioning coaches, designing programs to increase athletic performance, help prevent injuries and boost mental strength and confidence. In contrast, even today, coaches in combat sports often perpetuate old myths like, "Lifting will make you muscle bound and slow".

"As to methods there may be a million and then some, but principles are few. The man who grasps principles can successfully select his own methods. The man who tries methods, ignoring principles, is sure to have trouble."

— Harrington Emerson

The exact system outlined in this manual is not particularly important, but the principles it is built upon are extremely so. While many years of experimentation and lots of thought has gone into the development of this system, I have boiled it down to four basic principles that will be unpacked in further detail.

1. Minimalist Training
2. Hierarchy of Physical Attributes
3. Adaptability
4. Sustainability

The concept of minimalist training has been called many things: the minimax principle, minimum effective dose, the 80/20 principle, etc., but they all refer to the same idea that we should accomplish as much as possible in the least amount of time as possible while using the least amount of energy as possible. This is particularly important in combat sports training, especially MMA, which most of this manual will concern itself with. Skill is generally more important than strength in fighting. Anyone who has been around the fight game long enough knows that a fighter with significantly better technique can beat a superior athlete on a consistent basis, and most likely has a personal story of failure and humiliation involving rolling, clinching or wrestling with a smaller partner. I have experienced this on many occasions, from getting dominated by the 138-pound wrestler in my high-school wrestling room, to eating a mean body shot my first time boxing sparring, and then getting balled up on jiu-jitsu mats, and years later when I should have known better, I was still shocked by how easily small Thai boys in Bangkok tossed me in clinch training. Since strength is not the most important part of winning fights, it is of utmost importance to prioritize technical sport-specific training for combat athletes. If an MMA fighter has two pad sessions, three jiu-jitsu practices, a Muay Thai night, a wrestling session and sparring every week, they will inevitably have neither the time nor the energy to devote themselves to a bunch of long, drawn-out strength and conditioning sessions. A fighter should lift weights to be a better fighter, not a better lifter, and spend as much time as possible practicing their actual sport. This is a particularly important concept for non-skill coaches who exclusively run strength and conditioning practices.

Another reason that minimalist training is important for fighters is that excessive strength and conditioning is redundant considering all the other training they do. A combat athlete must be powerful, strong and mobile, as well as having good muscular and cardiovascular endurance. Striking sports can be a great way to develop power, grappling arts are a tried and true way to build muscular endurance, and both can contribute to specific types of mobility improvements. Pretty much all combat sports build serious cardiovascular endurance. Therefore, it is not always necessary to put an excessive amount of effort into developing these attributes. In Verkhoshansky and Siff's seminal book, Supertraining, they write: "Basic biomechanical analysis of the forces and tensions involved show clearly that the high levels of resistance and muscle tension involved in sports such as gymnastics, swimming, rowing and wrestling easily justify any objections to regarding resistance training as a separate training system" [1]. This is a long way of saying that the sport-specific skill training that wrestlers, or any other combat sport practitioners, do is a part of their strength and conditioning in and of itself. Because of these redundancies, this system appears to somewhat neglect high volume ab work that can be developed through punching or playing guard in jiu-jitsu, neck strengthening that is best developed through Thai clinching, grip strength from wrestling or rolling and basic levels of cardiovascular and muscular conditioning that all kinds of combat athletes should have from their sports.

So if combat sports are so great at developing athletic properties, what do we even need a weight room for? This answer will vary from sport to sport, for example, a pure boxer who is not clinching and wrestling will need to do some extra neck strengthening exercises, while a pure grappler may require more posture correcting mobility movements. These specific needs will be discussed in a later section, but what all combat sports require are high levels of full body power from explosive exercises, strength from heavy compound lifts and mobility, and stability and flexibility from smaller exercises, which will from here on be referred to as ancillary exercises. These ancillary exercises will help to correct issues that arise from fight training such as the decline in specific ranges of motion and the bad posture that sustained wrestling stances produce. Additionally, they act as a form of "prehab" to prevent these issues in the first place. A premium will be placed on scapular control, spinal extension and traction and hip mobility, although eccentric hamstring exercises, flexibility and extra neck or ab exercises will sometimes fall into the ancillary category. Extra conditioning drills will only be required when peaking for a fight. The hierarchy of physical attributes is as follows:

Movement Patterns > Strength > Power > Specialization

This is common sense for a good strength and conditioning coach, but it is important to bring one attribute up to a proficient level before focusing on the next. Building strength with faulty movement patterns will only lead to more problems down the line. Power is very tightly correlated to strength, so working on power development without a strength base is a waste of time. With that said, once an athlete is strong enough to effectively carry out the techniques in their sport, they will hit a point of diminishing returns regarding more strength work. If I take a fighter with a max deadlift of their own bodyweight and a max bench press of less than their bodyweight, which is surprisingly common among fighters, taking their deadlift up to double bodyweight and their bench press up above bodyweight will significantly improve their performance on the mats or in the ring or cage. Now taking that same fighter up to a triple bodyweight deadlift and an above double bodyweight bench press may improve their performance, but the training effort, recovery time and stress on the joints will almost certainly not be worth it. Specific guidelines will be discussed later, but it is important to know that although strength is the number one goal for athletes with proper movement patterns, there is a limit - and strong enough is strong enough. Once an effective amount of power has been developed, an athlete can specialize their training further, working to develop even more mobility, endurance or any other attribute they need.

The adaptability of this program allows a wide range of athletes to use the same system and training schedule, while meeting their individual needs and following the hierarchy outlined above. This system is not a set program so much as it is an outline with spaces for movements to be added in for each fighter. This means a team of athletes can all train together at the same pace and schedule while working on individual goals. For example, everyone will be doing a squatting movement at the same time, but one athlete may be doing goblet squats to build the movement pattern, while another is back squatting to maximize strength and another could be doing a unilateral version to restore balance between limbs after an injury. Between sets of the squats each fighter will do ancillary exercises that can also be adapted to each fighter's needs and limitations. Additionally, even if two athletes are performing the exact same exercises, different adaptations can be had by choosing an appropriate set and rep scheme for their goals and experience level. Details on exercise selection and set and rep schemes will be discussed in later chapters, but generally speaking this system will utilize low reps to build maximum strength and power while limiting hypertrophy to keep athletes in their weight class.

Sustainability of a strength and conditioning program is essential for fighters, since most fight sports do not have seasons and staying in shape year-round is necessary. The grueling nature of combat sports training means that total lifting volume and recovery must be well managed to lift year-round, but the benefits of doing so are immense. For one, an athlete will not have to "get in shape" in the months leading up to a fight. They simply get into peak condition while still having time and energy for skill work. Second, big opportunities in the career of a fighter can present themselves in the form of short-notice fights. Being prepared for those opportunities could be the difference between moving into a larger organization with more eminence and pay or staying at a regional or local level. What makes this system sustainable long term are the low training volumes and limited eccentric work, which also help reduce hypertrophy and delayed onset muscle soreness (DOMS), and the scheduled deload or rest weeks, which gives the athlete time to recover.

Before anything else can be accomplished, a coach must have an athlete buy into their methods to successfully train them. Teaching the athletes who you train these overriding principles is essential, so they understand the whys, not just the how's, of this system, which is not always easy since some of these principles conflict with traditional training methods. Plenty of elite fighters have won competitions despite what appears to be scientifically incorrect training from an outside perspective. As long as a fighter truly believes that they are doing the right thing and putting in hard work, they can overcome flawed training methods and perform well. So, teaching the principles and creating confidence in the system is the first step to improving performance with these methods.

— Chapter 2 —

Programing a Week and Cycle

Day One		**Day Two**	
A1 Power Hinge	3x3-5	A1 Power Squat	3x3-5
A2 Ancillary	3x8-12	A2 Ancillary	3x8-12
B1 Strength Hinge	3x3-5	B1 Strength Squat	3x3-5
B2 Ancillary	3x8-12	B2 Ancillary	3x8-12
C1 Vertical Press	3x3-5	C1 Horizontal Press	3x3-5
C2 Vertical Pull	3x8-12	C2 Horizontal Pull	3x8-12

Each week will contain two non-consecutive lifting days comprising a power movement, a lower body strength movement, ancillary exercises, and an upper body press and pull movement. These workouts are performed for three weeks, and then a deload week is taken, followed by three more weeks, another deload, and then all of the exercises are switched to prevent stagnation. This eight-week chunk is one cycle. Each cycle contains a "gymnastic press" movement, ring dips for example, for greater training variety and shoulder stability work. Also, an eccentric hamstring exercise, such as a Nordic hamstring curl, is included to help prevent injuries to the knee and hamstring. In a 2016 review of 19 studies, a decrease in the risk factors of ACL and hamstring injuries was seen when an eccentric hamstring injury prevention protocol was followed [2]. These hamstring exercises can be programmed as an ancillary exercise after the power and leg strength exercises or as a power movement, such as a kettlebell swing, that includes eccentric hamstring work in its nature.

Most power exercises, all lower body exercises and most upper body pressing are done within the three to five repetition range. The exceptions are certain kettlebell power exercises that can safely be pushed into higher reps and gymnastic presses where the focus is on sustained tension and stability. This low rep range ensures maximum power output and safety for the plyos and O-lifts, and an emphasis on max strength, without excess hypertrophy, for the leg and pressing lifts. If possible, drop weights and take all safe measures to limit eccentric work, which can lead to excess hypertrophy and DOMS. Some kettlebell power exercises, most ancillary movements and upper body pulls are performed in the eight to twelve repetition range. Only kettlebell movements that the athlete feels comfortable with should be pushed up into this higher range and it is absolutely fine to keep the reps lower. Ancillary movements are usually mobility or stability based, such as hip circles or Pallof presses, and require a bit more time under tension along with higher reps, although some ancillaries, such as static stretches or kettlebell armbars, can be timed or performed for lower reps. Upper body pulls use a higher rep range for a couple of reasons. First, I like the powerlifting idea that the back should be built up as a base for pressing to be performed off of. Second, most upper body pulling in combat sports is to control your opponent's posture or squeeze a submission, both requiring more muscular endurance than pure strength. It could be argued that pulling your hand back after throwing a punch is not a slow or controlling pull, but it is also a very sport-specific movement pattern, which has no business being trained in the weight room. Exact loading schemes will be discussed in-depth in Chapter 4.

— Chapter 3 —

Exercise Selection

Each exercise should be selected to fit the structure of the system, but also your athlete's skill level, past lifting cycles and other personal limitations or needs. For example, if you have an athlete who has never lifted before, they probably should not be doing heavy snatches on their first day. First teach them to hip hinge, create full body tension, deadlift, triple extension, etc. If you are at the end of a cycle and have a fighter who is experiencing great strength gains in the back squat, it may be a good idea to switch to a box squat or something similar, so they stay excited about training. If you have a wrestler with the wear-and-tear of thousands of matches who is transitioning to MMA, and their body is so beat up to the point that they cannot squat without their knees knocking and heels lifting off the ground, then it is not a great idea to start heavy back squats. Instead, have them do light goblet squats for movement quality, not high load. What makes this program so adaptable is that regardless of an athlete's skill level or needs, a good coach will be able to program appropriately while still maintaining the basic structure. This means you can easily keep a group of fighters on the same lifting cycle, lining up schedules and deload weeks, while meeting each athlete's needs. An experienced coach should know each athlete's needs, but when in doubt refer to the hierarchy of physical attributes.

Movement Patterns > Strength > Power > Specialization

Now we will break down each day, movement by movement to construct a coherent sample plan for a fighter new to lifting, as well as a more advanced athlete. For a list of exercises that can be substituted into the program, see the movement tables supplied at the end.

I do not believe a warmup needs to be particularly long or complicated. The only specific drill I insist that my fighters do before a training session is to roll out their ankles, especially before plyos. Personally, the majority of the time I just warm up with a few light sets of my first exercise, with a few unstructured stretches or mobility movements that feel right. However, here are a few sample warmups that can be used for a bit more structure.

PVC Pipe Warmup - Excellent for cycles with lots of barbell movements. Do each exercise for about 30 seconds and repeat if necessary.

   A1 **PVC Dislocates**

   A2 **PVC Hinges** with pipe touching the back of the head, T spine and tailbone through full hinge

   A3 **PVC Overhead Squat**

   A4 **PVC Bradford Press**

Kettlebell Warmup - Short and sweet. Can be completed with one kettlebell. Repeat until warm.

A1 **Prying Goblet Squat**   x10
A2 **Halos**   x5 each direction
A3 **Swings**   x10

Joint Mobility Warmup - I have fighters perform this before fights and particularly hard practices that will involve unusual positions, like hard grappling or shoot boxing, and it works well to prepare the body for lifting especially in tighter athletes who lack mobility. Do each exercise for about 30 seconds.

A1 **Ankle Rolls** – Put weight on the ball of one foot and grip the floor with the toes. Make a circle with the heel to take the ankle through a full range of motion. Reverse direction, and then repeat on the other side.

A2 **Knee Circles** – Stand with the feet and knees together. Circle the knees, starting small and working to larger circles. Repeat going in the other direction.

A3 **Hip Circles** – Starting either standing or on the hands and knees, take a knee forward, and then out and around in as large of a circle as possible without rotating the hips. Repeat going in the other direction, then on the other side.

A4 **Trunk Rotations** – Stand tall, rotate through the spine in each direction, looking over the shoulder on the side you rotated to.

A5 **Shoulder Circles** – Stand tall with the arms straight and rotate at the shoulder making small circles and slowly working to large circles. Repeat going in the other direction.

A6 **Elbow Circles** – Rotate at the elbows making large circles with your forearms. Repeat going in the other direction.

A7 **Neck Circles** – Make the biggest circle possible with the top of your head keeping the torso and shoulders still. Repeat going in the other direction.

On day one, after the light general warmup, we start with a power hinge movement, while the nervous system is still fresh. This includes any explosive movement that is primarily focused on the hip extensors, including plyometric exercises, kettlebell movements and Olympic lifts. The spectrum of complexity for these exercises is absolutely massive, and it is fine to use exercises anywhere on this spectrum as long as they are appropriately matched to the athlete's skill level and recovery abilities. Beginners can start with something as simple as a broad jump, while an experienced athlete can use any variation of cleans or snatches. Generally, I like to use a simple power exercise, like the broad jump, as a potentiation exercise for heavier strength movements, like deadlifts. The more complex and easier to load power hinge exercises, like Olympic lifts, I tend to use as the "main lift", followed by a strength movement requiring a relatively smaller load, such as good mornings or unilateral RDLs. It is also important to note that the eccentric hamstring exercise requirement can be met with properly performed kettlebell swings, where the athlete is actively throwing their bell down from the top of their swing, or controlled RDLs. For more advanced athletes who already move well, a plyometric power movement can be performed as a superset with the strength hinge movement first, which I will use in this example. This technique is called complex training, notably used by elite sprinting coach Barry Ross. However, I'd suggest not running consecutive cycles of complex training because it takes away spots for ancillary movements. The start of a sample workout would look like this:

Day One (Beginner)

A1 Kettlebell Swing*   3x5-10

Fulfills the eccentric hamstring exercise requirement

Day One (Advanced)

A1 Strength Hinge   3x3-5

A2 Broad Jump   3x3-5

Next, we will add a strength hinge movement, which should again be primarily focused on the hip extensors, and maximum loading potential. If the power hinge creates a lot of neural fatigue or an athlete is coming off an injury, a coach may use good mornings, GHDs, unilateral hinge movements or other lower intensity exercises, but for the most part this is where we want to go heavy and have the ability to progressively overload the movement over the course of the eight-week cycle. Deadlifts and their variations, like RDLs and trap bar deadlifts, should be the go-to picks. Be mindful of your athlete's ability to maintain a neutral spine in the bottom position. Rack pulls and pulling from the high handles on a trap bar are absolutely fine if your fighter lacks the mobility to stay safe throughout the full range of motion, although increasing that mobility should then become a primary goal with the ancillary exercises. Additionally, the concentric portion of the lift should be emphasized. While still not fully understood, some studies suggest that DOMS seem to be at least partially due to eccentric exercises [3]. For this reason, I always have my fighters use a "controlled drop" from the top of their deadlifts, and literally drop the bar after their last rep. While this may seem contradictory with the mandatory inclusion of eccentric hamstring exercises for injury prevention, the idea is to minimize eccentric work when possible, especially on large movements like deadlifts that can cause soreness throughout the whole body and affect skill workouts later in the week. Adding the strength movement into our sample day one workout looks like this:

Day One (Beginner)

A1 Kettlebell Swing*	3x5-10
A2 Ancillary	3x8-12
B1 Trap Bar Deadlift	3x3-5
B2 Ancillary	3x8-12

*Fulfills the eccentric hamstring exercise requirement

Day One (Advanced)

A1 Deadlift	3x3-5
A2 Broad Jump	3x3-5
A3 Ancillary	3x8-12

So far we have glossed over the ancillary exercises, so it is time to add some detail and put specific movements into our sample program. Ancillary exercises are used to increase or maintain mobility and stability in weak areas, improve combat sport-related decreases in posture and ensure that overzealous fighters will take a sufficient rest between heavy strength and power sets. After each set of a main lift, a different ancillary is used so that a wider variety can be fit within the structure of the workout. Despite the broad range of movements that can be used as an ancillary exercise, it is important not to treat them as random time wasters. Each movement should be used for a specific purpose based on a fighter's needs. Based on the needs of combat sport athletes, strengthening and increasing mobility throughout the shoulder girdle, spine and hips should take priority. However, additional abdominal or neck strengthening, or flexibility drills or eccentric hamstring exercises, which do not fit into the power hinge category, can be added too.

If needed, even more specific goals can be met by addressing one issue with each ancillary exercise. For example, I had a fighter who was working on a lot of elbows from top guard and mount because of his excellent wrestling ability. However, his shoulder mobility was so bad that he could not go through a large enough range of motion to break grips and throw an elbow with power. For almost six months most of his ancillary exercises involved increasing his range of motion in the glenohumeral joint and strengthening the rotator cuff and scapular control muscles with dislocates, wall slides, kettlebell armbars, windmills, facepulls, scapular pushups, hang stretches and other exercises of the sort. He and his other coaches were extremely impressed with his progress after this relatively small period of time and he has since landed some monstrous elbows in fights. This significant increase in range of motion is all because of a few well-programed and executed exercises performed twice a week between heavy sets, instead of just sitting around.

It is also important that the ancillary exercises selected will not have a negative effect on the main lift. For example, if you wanted to use Nordic hamstring curls as an eccentric hamstring exercise in a cycle with cleans and deadlifts, it should be programmed in after the last heavy set of deadlifts, so as not to interfere. Adding specific ancillary exercises into our sample day one workout looks like this:

Day One (Beginner)

A1 Kettlebell Swing*	3x5-10
A2 Facepull	1x12
Yoga Bridge	1x10sec
Hip Flexor Stretch	1x30sec
B1 Trap Bar Deadlift	3x3-5
B2 KB Armbar	1x3/side
Scapular Push-Up	1x10
Pallof Press	1x12/side

Day One (Advanced)

A1 Deadlift	3x3-5
A2 Broad Jump	3x3-5
A3 Windmill	1x6/side
T-Spine Rotations	1x30sec
Nordic Ham Curl*	1x8

*Fulfills the eccentric hamstring exercise requirement

For a large list of effective ancillary movements I commonly use with my fighters, see the tables at the end of this manual. However, ancillary movement slots are the easiest place to add in new exercises and drills, so feel free to implement whatever mobility, stability, balance, prehab, etc. movements you like, so long as they fit within the structure of the system.

At this point in the workout we have completed the more taxing lower body movements as well as the ancillary exercises, so it is time to program in the upper body vertical push and pull exercises. There are a few things to keep in mind as we select pressing exercises. One of the pressing exercises in the week must be a gymnastic press and, while breaking down the pressing into vertical and horizontal movements is a good guideline, it will not always work out exactly like that. For example, in one cycle you could combine ring dips with an incline barbell press, and they would be effective while not being exactly horizontal and vertical. What is most important is that one pressing exercise in the week occurs in a significantly different plane than the other day. As a rule of thumb, you should try to have the pressing exercises occur in planes that are at least 90° apart. For example, a dumbbell bench press could be combined with handstand pushups in one cycle, while a military press and handstand pushups are too similar in nature and would result in a cycle that neglects pressing at a lower angle.

Another important aspect of programming pressing movements is the type of resistance used. Single arm pushups, barbell bench presses and dumbbell bench presses all move across a similar plane, but will accomplish different goals. What you choose will be affected by the athlete's goal, what tools you have available and also personal preference. In general, barbell presses will increase maximum strength faster, while dumbbell, kettlebell and single arm presses will help even out strength imbalances. I try to alternate between different types of tools to reap a wider variety of benefits, but it is totally fine to run a few cycles in a row using similar tools if they help an athlete attack a specific goal. If you have an overall weak fighter, running multiple cycles of barbell pressing will help them gain more strength with the higher total loads, while a grizzled vet with one screwy shoulder can absolutely run as many cycles as needed using dumbbells, kettlebells and single arm presses to help gain a better range of motion and help prevent further asymmetries.

Gymnastic presses are used because of their excellent ability to increase stability within the shoulder girdle, full body tension and control, and to increase exercise variety. Be sure to use appropriate exercises and regressions based on the athlete's skill level. Some of these regressions will be included in the gymnastic pressing exercise table at the end of this section.

Vertical pulls should almost always be pull-ups, chin-ups and all their variations. I encourage my fighters to try out different grips, hand positions, tempos and body positions each set to help avoid any overuse injuries and give the individual more control over their program. I have athletes, who cannot quite perform sets of 8 to 12 good reps, alternate weekly between using a band for assistance and eccentric-only reps. Every once in a while, I have the fighters use additional weight and let them drop the reps a (fairly arbitrary) "little bit". Although stricter loading schemes can be applied to the pull/chin-ups, I believe this is a great place not to overthink and micromanage, and just get the work in. Adding in our vertical push and pull and finishing up day one looks like this:

Day One (Beginner)

A1 Kettlebell Swing*	3x5-10
A2 Facepull	1x12
Yoga Bridge	1x10sec
Hip Flexor Stretch	1x30sec
B1 Trap Bar Deadlift	3x3-5
B2 KB Armbar	1x3/side
Scapular Push-Up	1x10
Pallof Press	1x12/side
C1 One Arm KB Press	3x3-5/side
C2 Pull/Chin-Up	3x8-12

Fulfills the eccentric hamstring exercise requirement

Day One (Advanced)

A1 Deadlift	3x3-5
A2 Broad Jump	3x3-5
A3 Windmill	1x6 side
T-Spine Rotations	1x30sec
Nordic Ham Curl*	1x8
B1 Handstand PU**	3x8-12
B2 Pull/Chin-Up	3x8-12

Fulfills the eccentric hamstring exercise requirement

**Fulfills the gymnastic press requirement*

On day two, after the light general warmup, we start with a power squat movement, while the nervous system is still fresh. This includes any explosive exercise focusing on the quadriceps. While plyometric exercises, such as squat jumps and box jumps, are great, try to also cycle in some jumps from a static position with no loading or eccentric phase. I believe training power movements without relying on the increased muscle potentiation, stretch reflex and elasticity of filaments in the muscle and tendon from a true plyometric exercise, can help a fighter perform explosive techniques, such as a kick or blast double, without telegraphing as much. With that said, punches and takedowns are often used off of slips, rock backs and while circling, taking advantage of the loading phases present in a fighter's natural movement. Therefore, there is no need to switch entirely to non-plyometric power exercises.

While learning proper exercise technique is beyond the scope of this manual, be exceptionally careful with advanced movements like multiple box jumps and depth jumps. I consider them to be some of the most dangerous exercises that I have my fighters do. This is what the start of day two looks like:

Day Two (Beginner)

A1 Squat Jump 3x3-5

Day Two (Advanced)

A1 Depth Jump 3x3-5

Our ancillary exercises on day two will follow the same guidelines as before. Notice the ancillaries are primarily to mobilize the hips and ankles, as well as engage in some full body tension in the beginner example, specifically preparing the body for the following squat movement. With the ancillaries added, our program looks like this:

Day Two (Beginner)		**Day Two** (Advanced)	
A1 Squat Jump	3x3-5	A1 Depth Jump	3x3-5
A2 Hip Circles	1x3/ leg	A2 Roll IT Band	1x30sec
Hip Flexor Stretch	1x30sec	Piriformis Stretch	1x30sec
Ab Wheel	1x10	Calf Stretch	1x30sec

Next up is our strength squat movement, which should primarily focus on knee extension, while allowing for maximum loading potential. Generally speaking, bilateral barbell squat variations will allow for greater overall loading and strength gains, while unilateral options are great for evening strength imbalances, diagnosing improper movement patterns and reducing overall loading, which is great for veteran fighters who are a bit beat up from years of hard training. To get all the benefits from both types of movements I alternate between programming bilateral and unilateral squat variations every few cycles. Adding the strength squat movement and the ancillaries to be superset with it looks like this:

Day Two (Beginner)		**Day Two** (Advanced)	
A1 Squat Jump	3x3-5	A1 Depth Jump	3x3-5
A2 Hip Circles	1x3/ leg	A2 Roll IT Band	1x30sec
Hip Flexor Stretch	1x30sec	Piriformis Stretch	1x30sec
Ab Wheel	1x10	Calf Stretch	1x30sec
B1 Goblet Squat	3x3-5	B1 Weighted Pistol	3x3-5
B2 Pull Apart	1x12	B2 IYT	1x12
T-Spine Rotations	1x3/side	Dislocates	1x10
Hang Stretch	1x30sec	Barbell Rollouts	1x10

The only thing left for our day two lift is to add a horizontal upper body press and pull. Any variation of bench presses or pushups are great options for the press. I tend to limit barbell bench pressing in favor of dumbbell bench presses to ensure more symmetrical strength gains, improve shoulder stability and help avoid nagging shoulder soreness, which I find many fighters already have on a regular basis. As with the pull/chin-ups, I encourage my fighters to vary their grips with their rows, not only between pronated, neutral and supinated, but also the bar thickness. Finishing out our sample day two workout looks like this:

Day Two (Beginner)		**Day Two** (Advanced)	
A1 Squat Jump	3x3-5	A1 Depth Jump	3x3-5
A2 Hip Circles	1x3/leg	A2 Roll IT Band	1x30 secs
Hip Flexor Stretch	1x30 secs	Piriformis Stretch	1x30 secs
Ab Wheel	1x10	Calf Stretch	1x30 secs
B1 Goblet Squat	3x3-5	B1 Weighted Pistol	3x3-5
B2 Pull Apart	1x1	B2 IYT	1x12
T-Spine Rotations	1x3/side	Dislocates	1x10
Hang Stretch	1x30 secs	Barbell Rollouts	1x10
C1 Single Arm PU**	3x3-5	C1 DB Bench Press	3x3-5
C2 TRX Row	3x8-12	C2 Barbell Row	3x8-12

** Fulfills gymnastic press requirement

    This fully programmed week of training will be repeated for three weeks, with a deload on the fourth week. For the deload there are several options: lower the weights to about 50% and do the same workout, replace the lift with yoga/restorative ancillary exercises/light movements, teach the new lifts from the next cycle or better yet have the fighters stay out of the weight room altogether and roll, hit mitts or just rest. Regardless of the type of deload used, the athlete should feel better after the deload workout than when they walked into the gym. Personally, I like to give my fighters a week off from being in the weight room, but a sample light movement deload workout will be given below. After the deload, do three more weeks with the same exercises and then another deload, which makes up one full cycle. After the end of the cycle, assess what worked and what did not, select new exercises and repeat the process. This can be continued year-round until a fight is scheduled and the peaking process, which will be discussed in a later chapter, begins.

Sample Deload Workout

A1 Dislocates with PVC	2x10
A2 Hinge with PVC on tailbone, T-spine and back of the head	2x10
A3 Overhead Squat with PVC	2x10
B1 Kettlebell Halo	2x5/each way
B2 Kettlebell Windmill	2x5/each side
B3 Band Facepulls	2x15
C1 RKC Plank	2x15 secs
C2 Band Pallof Press	2x10/side
C3 T-Spine Rotations with Side Crunch	2x2 secs/side
D1 Hip Circles	x5 both directions/sides
E1 Roll Hamstrings, IT Bands and Quads	x45 secs each
F1 Stretch Hamstrings, Quads, Hip Flexors and Piriformis	x30-60 secs each
G1 Hang Stretch	x60 secs

— Chapter 4 —

Loading Schemes

The loading scheme used must be selected for each athlete's training experience and goals. The following examples should usually only be used for the strength hinge, strength squat, upper body pressing and some of the weighted power exercises. The exact reps do not matter nearly as much with the gymnastic presses, upper body pulling and ancillary exercises as long as a proper technique is utilized. I do not care if an athlete does 10 or 12 facepulls, one arm pushups or rows, as long as the technique is acceptable and, over the course of the cycle, the quality, intensity and volume (in that order) are improved upon. While there are a ton of ways to program for the heavy exercises performed in the three to five rep range, the following four periodization methods are the ones I have personally used with my athletes to great success.

Linear

This type of periodization consists of increasing load or reps each and every training session and works especially well for new lifters. It is not a great option for more advanced lifters who are already near their maximum strength levels and can lead to frustration and overtraining. With newer lifters, I like to have them do three sets of five reps on an exercise, increasing the load each set. As long as all of the reps are completed with good technique, at the following training session their first work set will be carried out with the load used on their second set from the previous session. This process is repeated for the duration of the cycle, though the increases in load may not be as large the further into the cycle you go. If a rep is missed or the lifting technique is unacceptable, the following week use the same loads or slightly less, and try to complete all of the reps. An example cycle for a beginner lifter using the front squat is shown below. Notice the slowing of progression deeper into the cycle. This is why this simple type of linear periodization cannot be used for long periods of time, or for more advanced lifters. Also note that the deload weeks still involve front squatting and that the load is more than the 50% decrease I suggested before. For new lifters this is acceptable, so they can continue to develop the skill of front squatting and the load is still low enough not to cause excessive fatigue on the nervous system.

Week 1: Front Squat
    Set 1: 95lbs x 5   Set 2: 115lbs x 5   Set 3: 135lbs x 5

Week 2: Front Squat
    Set 1: 115lbs x 5   Set 2: 135lbs x 5   Set 3: 155lbs x 5

Week 3: Front Squat
    Set 1: 135lbs x 5   Set 2: 155lbs x 5   Set 3: 165lbs x 5

Week 4: Front Squat Deload
    Set 1: 95lbs x 5   Set 2: 95lbs x 5   Set 3: 95lbs x 5

Week 5: Front Squat
    Set 1: 155lbs x 5   Set 2: 165lbs x 5   Set 3: 175lbs x 5

Week 6: Front Squat
    Set 1: 165lbs x 5   Set 2: 175lbs x 5   Set 3: 185lbs x 4

Week 7: Front Squat
    Set 1: 165lbs x 5   Set 2: 175lbs x 5   Set 3: 185lbs x 5

Week 8: Front Squat Deload
    Set 1: 115lbs x 5   Set 2: 115lbs x 5   Set 3: 115lbs x 5

Another option I use fairly often with new lifters, which can occasionally be used by more advanced ones as well, is the 3-4-5 method. The first week, work up to a comfortable triple. It is vital not to go too heavy at the start. The athlete should only work up to a weight that they feel they could hit even if they were tired or feeling "off" that day. The next training session they will do three sets of three reps at that weight. As long as all of the reps were performed well, during the next session the athlete will do three sets of four reps with the same weight. As long as all of the reps were performed well, during the next session the athlete will do three sets of five reps with the same weight. Then, assuming all of the reps were performed well, during the next session the athlete will do three sets of three reps with a higher weight, generally 10 to 20lbs for lower body lifts and 5 to 10lbs for upper body lifts, and the process continues. If a rep is missed, during the following training session use the same weights, or slightly less, and try to hit the same amount of reps. An example cycle using front squats is shown on the next page.

Week 1: Front Squat
    Set 1: 135lbs x 3   Set 2: 155lbs x 3   Set 3: 185lbs x 3

Week 2: Front Squat
    Set 1: 185lbs x 3   Set 2: 185lbs x 3   Set 3: 185lbs x 3

Week 3: Front Squat
    Set 1: 185lbs x 4   Set 2: 185lbs x 4   Set 3: 185lbs x 4

Week 4: Off Week Deload
    Fighter does some skill work, light mobility, or just rests

Week 5: Front Squat
    Set 1: 185lbs x 5   Set 2: 185lbs x 5   Set 3: 185lbs x 5

Week 6: Front Squat
    Set 1: 205lbs x 3   Set 2: 205lbs x 3   Set 3: 205lbs x 3

Week 7: Front Squat
    Set 1: 205lbs x 4   Set 2: 205lbs x 4   Set 3: 205lbs x 4

Week 8: Off Week Deload
    Fighter does some skill work, light mobility, or just rests

Autoregulated

An autoregulated loading scheme is similar to a percentage-based one, which is outlined next, except the percentages used are based on recent past performances instead of a true one rep max. This allows both newer lifters and more advanced ones to progress at an appropriate rate. This is the style of periodization I use most often with my athletes. Programming like this also self-corrects the load to the athlete's current state. If their performance falls because they have been doing significantly more training outside of the weight room or getting less sleep, the loads used will decrease. If they are eating and recovering better, the loads will increase. I first started experimenting with the 3RM and 6RM autoregulated programs outlined in Supertraining called APRE (autoregulating progressive resistance exercise). What I found was that the higher volume and hitting failure multiple times in one training session were too much for MMA fighters to recover from with the high amount of successive skill work they were doing. Almost all of them experienced decreases in lifting and mat performance over the course of an eight-week cycle. I have since adapted the program to a lower volume version, which is outlined below. This version only takes the last set to failure, which I define to my athletes as the point at which they feel they cannot complete a proper rep with the correct technique and speed, not true momentary muscular failure. For specific purposes, different percentages of the three rep max can be used instead of those I recommend. For example, a newer lifter is able to handle slightly higher percentages because their three rep max is pretty far away from its full potential. Also this system can be based off of a higher number of reps if it better suits the exercise or training goals, as is the case with exercises like good mornings, where I do not want my athletes doing heavy triples, or if an athlete is focusing on hypertrophy to go up a weight class. However, for most of the strength and power exercises, the following loading scheme works very well. The three rep max can be tested in the first week or estimated, and by the end of the cycle it will have self-corrected. The loads for the first two sets are based on a percentage of the three rep max (3RM) and the last set is as many reps as FEEL GOOD. Remember we are not going to true momentary muscular failure. Depending on the amount of reps completed, the three rep max will be adjusted for the next training session based on the adjustment table below.

Set 1: 80% of 3RM x 3
Set 2: 90% of 3RM x 3
Set 3: 100% of 3RM x reps that feel good

Adjustment Table

Reps Completed in Set Three	Adjustment to 3RM for Next Session
1-2	10-20lbs less
3	No change
4+	10-20lbs more

An example cycle of what this loading scheme would look like for power cleans is outlined on the next page, where the first day the athlete works up to a three rep max and the percentages are based on that. Notice that the decreases in load are due to the quality and feel of the reps, not true missed reps, which I try my best to avoid with Olympic lifts and their variations. Also, in this example, power cleans are still done on the deload weeks because it is such a high skill lift and requires constant practice.

Week 1: Power Clean
    Set 1: 155lbs x 3   Set 2: 175lbs x 3   Set 3: 185lbs x 3
    New 3RM=185lbs

Week 2: Power Clean
    Set 1: 145lbs x 3   Set 2: 165lbs x 3   Set 3: 185lbs x 4
    New 3RM=195lbs

Week 3: Power Clean
    Set 1: 155lbs x 3   Set 2: 175lbs x 3   Set 3: 195lbs x 4
    New 3RM=205lbs

Week 4: Power Clean Deload
    Set 1: 95lbs x 3   Set 2: 95lbs x 3   Set 3: 95lbs x 3

Week 5: Power Clean
    Set 1: 165lbs x 3   Set 2: 185lbs x 3   Set 3: 205lbs x 2*
    New 3RM=195lbs

Week 6: Power Clean
    Set 1: 155lbs x 3   Set 2: 175lbs x 3   Set 3: 195lbs x 5
    New 3RM=205lbs

Week 7: Power Clean
    Set 1: 165lbs x 3   Set 2: 185lbs x 3   Set 3: 205lbs x 3
    New 3RM=215lbs

Week 8: Power Clean Deload
    Set 1: 105lbs x 3   Set 2: 105lbs x 3   Set 3: 105lbs x 3

Set stopped because bar speed felt too slow

Percentage Based

A percentage-based loading scheme is one in which the loads are prescribed as a percentage of a maximum lift, usually a one rep max. This type of programming is best for more advanced lifters who are already technically proficient in the exercises being used and who have developed a good amount of strength. This allows them to reference past performance and come up with a usable estimate for a one rep max instead of actually testing it. Percentage-based loading is not recommended for beginners since their one rep max will change so quickly that the loads prescribed will not get the desired training effect. For example, let's say you have an athlete who has learned how to goblet squat with good mechanics, so you progress them to barbell front squats. That day you test their one rep max and they can properly squat 185lbs. For the next week's workout, you want them to do sets of 80% for three reps, which is roughly 145lbs, and then at the following week's workout they do sets of 85% for three reps, which is roughly 155lbs. You are now three weeks into front squatting and what kind of progress do you see? How much do you think their one rep max has increased? Now imagine instead of one rep max testing this new lifter, which I would advise against anyways, you had them work up to a hard set of five and they get to 155lbs. For the next two weeks, instead of using percentages of that number, you progress linearly as outlined above. It is perfectly reasonable to assume that by the end of three weeks they could be hitting 175lbs for sets of five and getting significantly stronger than if they were playing around with lighter weights. With that said, when done correctly, percentage-based loading is great for advanced lifters who can become over-trained by hammering away with linear programming.

In my opinion, the gold standard for a percentage-based loading scheme is Jim Wendler's 5/3/1. I have used it personally and with my athletes for over seven years now and it has never failed to add strength while incorporating deloads at just the right time to avoiding overtraining. The first week, instead of three sets of five, I have my athletes work up to a heavy three to five rep max, then we use that to calculate an estimated one rep max to figure out loads for the rest of the cycle. I have no affiliation with Jim Wendler but would highly recommend that you buy his book and use his loading scheme in this system for your fighters who are more advanced lifters.

There is no example percentage-based loading scheme because the only time I use true percentage-based programs other than 5/3/1 are for special circumstances, such as an athlete returning from injury or peaking out. The former is outside the scope of this manual and the latter will be discussed in the peaking section. To avoid the issues with percentage-based loading outlined above, try using autoregulated loading, which is similar but more adaptable, or run a cycle of 5/3/1 with more advanced lifters.

Hypertrophy

Hypertrophy training should only be done when an athlete is moving up a weight class and it is of utmost importance to understand that the training is less important than the diet and recovery. If an athlete eats and sleeps enough, they could go up a weight class using the same low volume training methods discussed before. However, hypertrophy can be accelerated by changing up the loading schemes a bit. I would also advise using one of the previously outlined loading schemes, after the hypertrophy cycle is completed, but before competition, to build more strength at the larger size. There are a ton of creative loading schemes that grow muscle, and while I will only present a few options to tweak our normal rep ranges, just know you can really do whatever you want to increase the volume and intensity as long as it stays within common sense and the scaffolding of the program. Do not start doing extended sets of Olympic lifts, trade out a compound upper body press for tricep kickbacks or adding eight more sets to each exercise. The following loading scheme tweaks will add volume and intensity but still allow you to use decently heavy loads, build strength, put on some muscle while still only using three sets and the same exercises, which is great when lifting together in a group where not everyone is doing a hypertrophy cycle.

Power exercise reps:

Keep the reps low, in the three-to-five range. Upping the reps will change the nature of the exercise and can increase the risk of injury. Focus on keeping the technique solid and adding weight or increasing speed.

Lower body hinge and upper body press reps:

For these lifts I will give two options. Pick the appropriate one for each exercise and stick with it for the cycle.

1. Cluster sets – Pick a weight that the athlete can complete five good reps with. Do three reps, rest for about ten seconds, do three more reps, rest again for about ten seconds, and then finally do three more reps. The nine reps, or three clusters, is one set. Repeat for three total sets, and do not expect to get all nine total reps for each set at first. Once the fighter can complete all three sets of clusters, up the weight an appropriate amount and repeat.

2. Drop sets – Perform the sets as usual, but up the reps into the eight-to-ten range, reducing the load as little as possible. On the last set, after the last rep has been performed, immediately drop the weight down 20 to 40% and continue the exercise to momentary muscular failure. Be sure to use good spotters.

Squat reps:

The following tweak is partially tradition, partially bro science and, of course, largely backed by real science that shows a correlation between volume and hypertrophy [4]. The first set of squats will be a heavy set of ten reps. The second and third will be moderately heavy sets of 20 to 30 reps. Be sure to keep the weight high enough that these sets are miserable, or you will not get the desired growth. High rep squats should definitely be the hardest part of the hypertrophy cycle. Each week either add weight or reps to at least one of the sets. This extended time under tension will result in serious muscle growth, and the misery will boost mental fortitude.

Gymnastic press, upper body pulls and ancillary reps:

For the most part the rep ranges will stay the same, in the eight-to-12 range. The only changes, which are totally optional, are to add a few select heavier exercises as ancillaries or add a drop set on an upper body pull. Before changing an ancillary exercise to a bodybuilding style movement, be sure your athlete moves well enough to skip an opportunity to do a mobility drill. If the fighter does not already have good scapular, thoracic spine and hip mobility, stick to exercises that will improve those. Assuming the athlete's mobility is at an acceptable level, pick an exercise that will not interfere too much with the next exercises and can be loaded fairly heavy, and then program a set of it as an ancillary exercise. Examples of acceptable exercises are pullovers, barbell curls, skullcrushers or close grip bench presses. If you would like to add a drop set to pullups or rows, follow the protocol outlined above.

An example week of a hypertrophy cycle is below:

Day One		**Day Two**	
A1 Snatch High Pull	3x3-5	A1 Box Jump	3x3-5
A2 Dislocates	1x10	A2 Lateral Band Walk	1x10
KB Armbar	1x3/side	Hip Circles	1x3/side
BB Curl	1x12	Hip Flexor Stretch	1x30 sec
B1 RDL	3x3+3+3	B1 Back Squat	3x10,25,25
B2 Facepull	1x12	B2 TRX Ys	1x12
Prone Behind-Neck Press	1x12	Nordic Ham Curl	1x10
Ab Wheel	1x12	DB Pullover	1x12
C1 Overhead Press	3x8-10+dropset	C1 Ring Dips	3x8-12
C2 Chin/ Pullup	3x8-12	C2 Barbell Row	3x8-12

— Chapter 5 —

Strength Benchmarks

Everyone wants to know how strong they should be after x amount of time strength training in order to be a better fighter. This is a very difficult question, and honestly one without any perfect answers, which is admittedly kind of a cop out for someone who preaches that "strong enough is strong enough" for combat sports athletes. First of all, a fighter must be able to move well before worrying about adding strength as is outlined in the hierarchy of physical attributes. A beat-up veteran of the fight game who cannot squat with their heels on the ground and knees out will get more out of using a cycle to focus on ancillaries and goblet squats to build proper mobility and squat mechanics than struggling to add a few pounds to their squat at the expense of their MCLs. Second, technique is so important in combat sports that it is difficult to say how much exact strength improvements will carry over to a fighter's ability to shoot, sprawl, punch, kick, squeeze submissions, etc. Third, the anthropometry of fighters varies so much that it is impossible to give accurate guidelines for every exercise. A long-limbed fighter may be able to rip heavy deadlifts no problem, but get crushed under the bar when squatting, while a fighter with a stockier "hammer" body type may struggle with deadlifts due to short arms, but squat like a champ. This is all a long way of saying that the strength benchmarks provided are imperfect, but good goals for MOST combat sport athletes. Some athletes, coaches and pretty much any powerlifter will laugh at how easy these benchmarks are to hit, while some fighters will struggle to ever reach them. With that long-winded preface out of the way, the following benchmarks are where I have seen most fighters begin to gain a tangible carryover of strength to their sport. All loads are for a single one rep max unless otherwise specified.

Deadlift	Double bodyweight
Back Squat	Bodyweight for at least 10 reps
Pistol	Light dumbbells (5 to 10lbs) for at least 3 reps per leg
Bench Press	Bodyweight
Overhead Press	80% of bodyweight
Ring Dip	10 controlled reps
Pullup	10 controlled reps

Another measure of how strong a fighter must be is in relation to themselves. According to Heather Linden DPT from the UFC Performance Institute, for unilateral exercises the difference in an athlete's strength between sides should be less than 10%, or they are at an increased risk of injury. Good coaches should be able to use unilateral exercises as a diagnostic tool in this way. The strength ratios between anterior and posterior strength are also important. While I do not have an exact ratio to avoid injury, I have never personally seen anyone who has too much posterior strength. If an athlete squats significantly more weight than they can deadlift, pay close attention to their movement patterns. They most likely do not properly engage the posterior chain and often "squat their deadlift". Take a cycle to improve their movement patterns and increase their posterior chain strength.

— Chapter 6 —

Peaking

The most important aspect of the peaking process in regards to strength training is to keep in mind that a fighter will have even less energy than normal to devote to resistance training. There will be extra conditioning and skill work to do and probably weight to lose, depending on how far above fight weight your athlete walks around at. At this point your fighter should have developed an adequate level of strength, so the goal over the four-week peaking process is to gradually and methodically convert that strength into as much power as possible, without excessively draining workouts. While a base level of conditioning should be present year-round, additional extra conditioning workouts will be added. Ideally, they should be run by a skill coach, but a few options for conditioning workouts that can be done in the weight room will be presented.

The four-week peaking cycle will consist of a strength-speed week and a speed-strength week, using the same lifts as the previous cycle, an explosive strength week, using plyometrics/shock training and throws, and a full week of rest. Ideally the peaking cycle begins the week after a deload. However, if the cycles do not line up perfectly the athlete can either take a deload week before beginning the peaking cycle, regardless of what week they are on in the previous cycle, or go right into it if they are feeling good physically. This is where a strength coach needs to be in touch with how hard their athletes are training and make a judgement call. I tend to err on the side of taking a deload or rest week before peaking, but judgement should be made on a case-by-case basis. The first two weeks can be skipped altogether if a fighter is in a situation that requires them to take a short-notice fight. I once had a fighter take a fight nine days out to move up to a bigger promotion. Luckily he had been lifting consistently, and with just one plyometric training session and a rest week he was ready to go and won that fight as an underdog against the top ranked fighter in that organization at the time.

 The strength-speed and speed-strength weeks will use the same exercises as the previous cycle to avoid wasting the time needed to teach the athlete new exercise techniques and so that a fairly accurate 1RM can be estimated based on their heaviest sets from previous weeks. Even if a full cycle has already been completed, continue using the same exercises for the peaking process.

 The strength-speed week workouts will look identical to the workouts from previous cycles, except the lower body strength exercises and upper body non-gymnastic press will be performed at 60 to 70% of the estimated 1RM for three sets of triples. Do not attempt an actual 1RM test, just use a calculator to get a rough idea. Be sure to instruct the fighter to accelerate the bar, dumbbell, or kettlebell as fast as possible. Bar speed is the goal.

The speed-strength week workouts will again repeat the same format, except the load on the lower body strength exercises and upper body non-gymnastic press will be dropped again to 40 to 50% of the estimated 1RM. Again, three sets of triples will be performed and instructing the fighter to maximize bar speed is of utmost importance.

The explosive strength week will comprise two training sessions with this format:

Day 1		**Day 2**	
A1 Vertical Bilateral Jump 3x5		A1 Horizontal Bilateral Jump	3x5
B1 Horizontal Unilateral Jump	3x5	B1 Vertical Unilateral Jump	3x5
C1 Rotational Med Ball Throw	3x5	C1 Rotational Med Ball Throw	3x5
D1 Explosive Upper Body Push	3x5	D1 Explosive Upper Body Push	3x5
D2 Explosive Upper Body Pull	3x5	D2 Explosive Upper Body Pull	3x5

An example of an explosive strength week for a well-conditioned experienced athlete would look like this:

Day 1		**Day 2**	
A1 Box Jump	3x5	A1 Depth Drop to Broad Jump	3x5
B1 Single Leg Broad Jump	3x5	B1 Single Leg Lateral Hurdle Jump	3x5
C1 Rotational Med Ball Throw	3x5	C1 Rotational Med Ball Throw	3x5
D1 Explosive Pushups	3x5	D1 Supine Med Ball Throw	3x5
D2 Explosive Pull-Ups	3x5	D2 Ring Muscle-Ups	3x5

While this should go without saying, be exceptionally careful with exercise selection this close to a competition. A fighter with no past lifting experience should not use depth jumps as an intro to plyometrics. Depth jumps in particular can be rough on the nervous system and should only be prescribed at the correct height to advanced athletes who will not try to one up their teammates. According to Donald Chu and Gregory Myer's book Plyometrics Dynamic Strength and Explosive Power, depth jumps should be done from a box "that lets the athlete maximize the height jumped and also achieve the shortest amortization phase" [5]. So if you see that your fighters are not bouncing off the floor quickly and jumping high, do not be afraid to tell them to use a shorter box.

After the explosive week, fight week begins and the fighter should stay out of the weight room, instead getting in a few light drilling, pad, and recovery sessions.

— Chapter 7 —

Conditioning

A fighter's conditioning should always be at a point in which they can comfortably spar for at least as many rounds as their fight, hit hard mitt rounds for at least a few more rounds than that and grapple for a long period of time. Obviously these are very subjective parameters, but as a coach you should have a rough idea of where your fighter needs to be to begin peaking for a fight. If you are exclusively a strength and conditioning coach, this is an essential time to be in contact with your fighter's skill coaches. They will have a much better idea of what kind of fight shape the athlete is in.

From this very important base level of conditioning, peaking to maximal levels is fairly straightforward and most of it should be done with a skill coach instead of a strength and conditioning coach only. Fight conditioning is just as much, if not more, about efficient movement and a calm mind than physiological adaptations, given that a fighter is at least in pretty good shape. Adding mental and emotional stress during conditioning drills, such as new people watching sparring, a designated trash talker during circuits, or visualizing walking out into a packed arena before training sessions, can greatly help a fighter overcome the sympathetic nervous system response during actual competition. While the rest of this chapter will focus on training for physiological adaptations, mental training will be covered more in depth in a later section.

Sparring should ramp up in intensity and by the last sparring session, usually a week out from fight week, the fighter should be able to be shark tanked for two rounds past what their fight length is. For example, if a fighter has an upcoming professional MMA fight that is the standard three, five-minute rounds, they should be able to spar five, five-minute rounds with a fresh partner each round. I suggest only sparring hard once a week when preparing for a fight, with drills and technical sparring one or two other times in the week. When an experienced fighter does not have a fight coming up, I believe sparring once a month or less is ideal, assuming they also have good drilling partners and pad holders. This allows for the development of proper timing and distance control without excessive brain trauma. These parameters are not set in stone, this is merely my opinion in a debate that has merit on all sides, and is quite frankly outside the scope of this strength and conditioning manual. However, regardless of whether you are a strength and conditioning coach, skill coach or training partner, please pay attention to, and point out, the signs of concussion in fighters, especially during the peaking process before a fight.

In addition to the normal lifting, skill work and sparring, fight-specific circuits should be introduced once or twice a week, roughly four weeks out from a fight, give or take one or two weeks depending on what kind of shape your fighter is already in. These circuits should start at the same number of rounds as the fight and work up to two rounds more than the fight. Using the example of a standard three, five-minute round MMA fight from earlier, at four weeks out, the athlete should be doing three, five-minute rounds. At three weeks out, they should do four, five-minute rounds. At two weeks out, they should do five, five-minute rounds. Fight week they should rest and just hit some pads or drill lightly. Like sparring frequency and intensity, this is where coaching is an art, not a science. Some fighters need more work to stay sharp mentally, while others may overtrain more easily. Learn from what has and has not worked for your athlete in the past leading up to a fight and pay attention to their ability to recover between training sessions. If their performance is dropping significantly, more rest may be necessary.

The fight-specific circuits should comprise various movements or drills that closely mimic what a fighter could encounter in their fight, while also maximizing power output. For example, hitting mitts, power punches on a soft medicine ball, power kicks on a bag, ground and pound on a bag, pummeling, standing up from turtle position with a partner on your back, drilling takedowns or sprawls and any other appropriate drill. These components should be alternated every 30 to 120 seconds. The selection of movements and drills to do, as well as the duration of each one, should be picked based on the specific fight coming up by the fighter's head coach. If you have an athlete whose biggest strength is striking and they are fighting a superior wrestler, it would make sense to include movements like standing up from the mat, sprawling and power punching as opposed to offensive wrestling and exotic kicks.

Two basic, but very effective examples of these fight-specific circuits that I personally used while boxing for Penn State, were alternating between power punching, constant speed punching and normal boxing on a bag for 30 seconds each for a full round, repeated for three to five rounds. The one I used most was alternating between burpees and shadow boxing every 30 seconds for a full round, repeated for three to five rounds. Now that I train primarily MMA fighters I still use this same concept for fight-specific circuits, although they have been greatly refined and coined as "fight sims" by MMA boxing coach extraordinaire Bob "The Stingray" Meese, who I have been lucky enough to work with while training some higher level fighters. An example of a fight sim for an MMA fighter would be a minute of hard pad work, followed by 30 seconds of takedown setups, then 30 seconds of ground and pound on a bag, then 30 seconds of power punching on a medicine ball held by a coach, repeated again for a five-minute round. After a minute of rest that round is repeated for a total of three to five rounds.

If, for whatever reason, a true fight sim cannot be carried out, the same principles can be utilized in a weight room using conditioning exercises such as sled pushes and pulls, rowing, ski ergometers, burpees, battle ropes, tire flips, weighted carries, etc.

Be sure the exercises are difficult, but not likely to make the fighter overly sore or put them at a high risk of injury. Peaking is not the right time to introduce high rep heavy squats, Olympic lifts or box jumps. A great example of a conditioning workout that can be done in the weight room, that I have personally seen work very well for fighters, is Bobby Maximus's Triathlon: 500m on the ski erg, then 50cal on the AirDyne, followed by a 500m row. One of my fighters decided he would never get tired again and, on his own accord, started doing the triathlon weekly during fight camp and before that I had never seen him in such great shape going into a fight.

Other combinations of exercises such as tire flips, med ball throws, burpees, sled pushing and pulling, etc. can be combined as well, just be sure the exercise selection is appropriate, and the intensity and duration are programmed to match up as closely as possible with the bioenergetic systems used in the fight. For example, an MMA fighter should do five minutes of work followed by a minute of rest three times, while a Muay Thai fighter should do three minutes of work followed by a minute of rest five times. On paper they look similar, 15 total minutes of work, but the rest periods will allow the Muay Thai fighter to up the intensity a bit, while the MMA fighter will be forced to tap further into their aerobic bioenergetic system.

— Chapter 8 —

Cutting Weight

Weight cutting may be the most vile and misunderstood part of the fight game. While I have felt absolutely heartbroken seeing my fighters get finished in big fights or being injured in training, nothing has hurt me more as a coach than seeing a fighter laying on the floor in agony, barely able to sweat anymore, telling that me that their organs hurt, all the while knowing they have to drop a few more pounds. What is worse is that even at high levels I have seen fighters and coaches go about the process of cutting weight completely wrong. I believe irresponsible weight cutting leads to serious long-term metabolic consequences that are not yet fully understood. For this reason, I would not suggest cutting weight at all for youth practitioners of combat sports, including high school wrestling.

A quick aside on weight cutting for women: The female endocrine system is more complex than that of their male counterparts and it requires higher body fat levels to stay healthy. Higher body fat percentages correspond to a lower percentage of water in the body, 45 to 50% for women as opposed to 50 to 60% in men. For this reason, I do not suggest chasing extremely low body fat percentages or cutting large amounts of weight. I have seen some women who can perform well and look fairly lean from as high as 24% and others as low as 15% body fat, so as long as performance is maximized do not worry too much about exact numbers. I will give some rough numbers for body fat percentages and weights in this section, but these numbers will NOT always apply to female fighters, who should focus on staying healthy and cutting the least amount of water weight possible.

Some fighters can get away with cutting no weight at all. Frankie Edgar was the UFC lightweight champion and only cut a few pounds. I recommend this to younger and lower level fighters and even higher level ones who can get away with it. Unfortunately, most serious fighters will have to cut some weight to stay competitive at their weight class. By cutting weight correctly, fighters should be able to cut enough to be the correct size for their weight class, while staying healthy enough to perform well and mitigate potential long-term damage. While exact cutting protocols will change based on the type of competition, when the weigh-ins are and the athlete themselves, there are a few principles that will apply across the board. These principles are to start the cut lean and light, control hormones and water retention, stay comfortable, be on weight for the least amount of time possible and rehydrate well.

Start the cut lean and light: Before cutting weight, a fighter should be lean, between seven and nine percent body fat, and fairly close to fight weight. If a fighter's body fat percentage is above 10% they must first lose weight before they can cut weight. Losing weight is a slower sustainable drop in body fat, which is not the same as a quick water cut, where the weight can easily be put back on. Because muscle tissue has a higher concentration of water than fat does, a leaner fighter will have more total water that they can cut, than their softer counterpart at the same weight. While each individual will be able to cut different amounts of weight and still perform well in a fight, as a rule of thumb, when a fighter is weighing in the same day as the fight, they should cut no more than five percent of their walking weight. Fighters weighing in the day before the fight should cut no more than 10% of their walking weight. Just to clarify, I do not recommend cutting this much weight, I only provide these numbers to give coaches and athletes an idea of how much weight is too much to cut safely. The following chart shows the absolute maximum weights that a fighter should begin cutting weight from for each of the current MMA weight classes.

Weight Class	Max Start Weight for Day of Weigh-ins	Max Start Weight for Day Before Weigh-ins
125	131.5	138.8
135	142.1	150
145	152.6	161.1
155	163.1	172.2
170	178.9	188.8
185	194.7	205.5
205	215.7	227.7
265	278.9	294.4

Control hormones and water retention: The human body maintains homeostasis via hormonal feedback loops, which we will take advantage of to cut weight. The main players in this balance of fluid retention are: vasopressin or antidiuretic hormone (ADH), which conserves water in the body, and the renin-angiotensin aldosterone system, which conserves sodium in the bloodstream, among other things. For simplicity we will focus on ADH, because it is easy to understand and manipulate, and if you are interested in physiology this is a good place to dive in. ADH is secreted when you are dehydrated and sodium concentrations in the bloodstream increase. ADH signals the kidneys to reabsorb water back into the bloodstream to retain plasma volume. Obviously we want to keep ADH levels as low as possible for as long as possible during the weight cut so the body does not try to conserve water and urine output remains high. To do this the fighter will drink a lot of water in the days leading up to the cut. Normally I have my fighters drink about a gallon of water a day, slightly more or less depending on their size. Then, on the Monday before the weigh-in they incrementally increase that to about two gallons a day up until the cut begins. Many coaches have their fighters taper off the water, drinking less and less the closer they get to the weight cut, but I believe that this is a counterproductive method. The more water my fighters have leading into a weight cut, the lower their ADH levels are, which means more water will be lost faster. Even during the weight cut, the first few times the fighter urinates it should be almost clear. Diet wise, sodium and carbs should be cut out about a day before the cut, as they lead to ADH secretion, thus water retention. The last meal before a cut starts should be a small amount of lean protein, for example, a 6oz chicken breast, and a big handful of veggies, with no sodium. I like my fighters to have lots of fibrous veggies leading up to the cut so they can still empty their bowels. One last note on controlling water retention: If your athlete takes creatine, which retains water in the body, have them stop four weeks out from competition to ensure creatine levels return to normal.

Stay comfortable(ish): While there is no way to totally avoid discomfort during a weight cut, the goal should be to stay as comfortable as possible. This means finding out what method of cutting works best for your fighter and not pushing them too hard. Most experienced fighters know if they want to use a sauna, steam room, or hot tub, and how much time they can tolerate in the heat. They will know if they want to actively work out or just sit passively. They will know when they will crave food or water and how to mitigate the cravings. For newer fighters who are less experienced it is worth doing a practice cut to figure all these things out. I recommend passively sweating in a hot tub, not staying in for more than 15 to 20 mins at a time, resting out of the tub for at least as long as you were in and to mitigate food and water cravings with gum or small bites of fruit.

Be on weight for the least amount of time possible: I have seen plenty of fighters start restricting water and wearing sauna suits during workouts many days before weigh-ins. As the body gets more and more dehydrated, it does a better job of holding on to the water it has (remember how ADH works), making a cut exponentially harder and more miserable the longer it is. My goal is to make the cut as quick and easy as possible to keep my athlete healthy and happy. I never have a fighter restrict fluids for more than 20 hours, and I prefer it to be less, especially for same day weigh-ins. The biggest reason fighters start cutting weight too early, 20+ hours out, is that they get scared of the number on the scale, especially if they are controlling their hormones properly by water loading up until it is time to cut, making them temporarily heavier.

Educate your athletes as to why they should stay hydrated for as long as possible and give them the opportunity to trust in this method. When to start the cut is a personal choice, and the more times a fighter cuts weight, the better idea you will have as to what time they should begin the cut. For athletes who do not have a ton of experience cutting weight, I would suggest beginning 20 hours out for day before weigh-ins and 16 hours out for day of weigh-ins. Eventually the goal should be to shorten the cutting time as much as possible, but testing the waters with a bit of extra time is good until you know for sure how fast a particular athlete cuts weight or, in the case of unforeseen hiccups, such as a hot tub or sauna that is not as hot as you would like, inaccurate scales or a fighter who decides to eat a bag full of grapes after they are already on weight.

Following is a sample schedule to cut weight for day before fight weigh ins, assuming the fight occurs on Saturday night as most MMA fights do. This example assumes there is too much weight to be lost entirely on the day of the weigh-ins, but if that is not the case by all means wait until the day of to cut and stay on weight for a smaller period of time.

Example Cut
Day Before Fight Weigh-ins at 5:00pm on Friday

Thursday 9:00pm (20 hours out) — Stop drinking water, but until 9:00pm keep water intake high to keep ADH low. 15 to 20 mins in a hot tub or sauna, followed by about 20 mins of recovery, wrapped in towels to stay warm and sweat. Urine should still be fairly clear after. The fighter should sleep in a warm room. By the end of the night the fighter should have dropped 30 to 50% of the total weight they need to cut. Gum can be chewed to avoid dry mouth and eating.

Friday 11:00am (6 hours out) — Eat one or two bites of fruit and/or a sip of coffee if needed. 15 to 20 mins in a hot tub or sauna, followed by about 20 mins of recovery, wrapped in towels to stay warm and sweat. Repeat if necessary. A coach should be within arm's reach of the athlete the whole time to monitor them. The athlete should be extra cautious when standing up as this is a large strain on the cardiovascular system when plasma volume has already been decreased and they could pass out. At this point the fighter should have dropped 70 to 80% of the total weight they need to cut.

Friday 3:00pm (2 hours out) — After a few hours of rest go back to 15 to 20 mins in a hot tub or sauna, followed by about 20 mins of recovery, wrapped in towels to stay warm and sweat. Repeat if necessary. Once on weight, head to the weigh-ins. As long as the fighter is not right on the brink of their weight limit, sucking on one or two ice cubes or having a small bite of fruit is acceptable to ease the misery.

Rehydrate well: The second the fighter is off the scale the rehydration process must begin. I have heard convincing arguments for many different substances to be used as the initial rehydration tool, but I think the most important thing is to try not to chug a lot of fluid at once, and constantly take in small amounts of fluid and food until the pre-cut weight has been put back on, the fighter feels good and is urinating clear. With that said, I would recommend water with a bit of sea salt, BCAAs and sugar or coconut water, and would avoid overly sugary sports drinks right away for a fighter stepping off the scale. By the time the faceoffs, handshakes and pictures have all been taken care of, the fighter should already have at least 10-20 ounces of fluid down, be feeling better and start snacking on fruit and continue drinking fluids. Remember the goal is not to eat massive quantities at once, but to consistently eat small amounts. For the next hour or two let the fighter rest, keep drinking fluids and have small snacks, preferably with sodium and potassium in them. At this point, if it is not against the rules and the fighter wants it, go ahead and use an IV to rehydrate, but at the higher levels this is often not allowed. When the fighter feels ready, they should have an actual meal without eating anything they have not eaten in the past few weeks. Be sure to have a good amount of healthy carbs such as potatoes or rice to replenish glycogen stores and help the fighter retain water. After the meal the fighter should already be at least as heavy as their pre-cut weight, and snacking and drinking fluids should continue as they feel comfortable and their urine should be clear. However, do not just chase scale weight by force-feeding. The fighter should feel comfortable.

— Chapter 9 —

Nutrition

Diet is extremely individual and quickly gets complex if you dig into the minutia. What works for one athlete may not work for another, and if you sift through studies, conflicting opinions run rampant. This section is not intended to be the definitive answer to what any one fighter's diet should be, but rather a "one-size-fits-most" set of guidelines for a simple, balanced and sustainable way to eat. The following principles are a great starting point for most athletes, but they are merely the tip of the iceberg. For more in-depth information on nutrition I would recommend reading one of the many books written entirely on nutrition. Better yet, work with a qualified sports nutritionist.

1. **Avoid extremes** - Nutrition advice and ideas swing like a pendulum over time. Currently low carb, high fat diets like paleo and keto are fairly popular, but do not forget that just a few decades ago fat, especially saturated fat, which is necessary for testosterone production, was considered the enemy of good health. Some fad diets certainly have their merits, but I would recommend that fighters try to keep their diets balanced to get all the macro and micronutrients they need to fuel intense

training. Any diet severely restricting a particular food group or macronutrient is probably not ideal for athletes.

2. **Drink lots of water** - This should go without saying, but a surprising amount of people, athletes included, do not get nearly enough water. Ask someone how much water they drink and they should be able to give you a rough amount. If they say "enough", "plenty", "I don't know" or the worst of all "eight glasses", then they do not drink enough water. As a rough rule of thumb, I tell non-fighters I train to drink at least 100oz of water a day, and fighters to drink at least a gallon (128oz) a day. Another easy metric to ensure proper hydration is to have athletes weigh in before and after practices. Any weight lost during the practice must be regained with water. An even easier way to ensure rehydration is to tell your athletes to drink water after training until their urine is clear. During training encourage your athletes to stay hydrated. It is one of the easiest ways to enhance high performance levels during hard practices and minimizes the amount they will need to drink to fully rehydrate afterwards. Sweat also contains electrolytes so adding salt to water is a good idea. No need to go crazy, just a little pinch that you should not be able to taste much if at all.

3. **Keep protein levels consistently high** - Protein is necessary to maintain muscle, which is obviously a top priority for a combat sport athlete. There is a lot of conflicting information

about how much protein people need, but I recommend somewhere between .7 and one gram of protein per pound of bodyweight, consumed fairly evenly throughout the day. Where that protein comes from is also important. Some sources of protein are incomplete, meaning they do not contain all the essential amino acids, and some are less bioavailable than others, meaning not all the protein in a particular food gets absorbed into your body. Generally speaking, with a few exceptions, animal sources of protein are complete, while plant sources are not. The research around protein can get really complex and is a great subject to dive into if you are interested in science and nutrition, but as long as you are getting most of your daily protein requirements from lean meats, fish, eggs and quality protein powder you will be just fine.

4. **Eat vegetables** - Eat lots of them and many different types - enough said.

5. **Fuel appropriately** - The human body uses both fatty acids and glucose (fat and carbs) for energy at any given time. However, during low intensity activities that can be sustained for long periods of time like walking, fat is prioritized as a fuel source, and during high intensity activities that cannot be sustained for a long time like wrestling, glucose is prioritized as a fuel source. In addition, the type of fuel ingested will also affect substrate use. So fatty acid oxidation, or the use of fat as

fuel, is increased when fats are primarily ingested and is quickly reduced when carbohydrates are ingested. What this means is that on top of the base of water, protein and vegetables, fats and carbs must be added in to match the type of training planned for that day as well as the body composition goals of the athlete. For example, a fighter who is two weeks out from a fight, already lean with single-digit body fat and is sparring in the evening, should have an afternoon meal with protein, some fat and a good amount of carbs, like a salmon fillet over rice with mixed vegetables on the side, to fuel their high intensity sparring. While a fighter who is a little soft at 14% body fat and plans on some very light jiu-jitsu drilling in the morning, may fuel their workout with protein and fat only, like an omelet with vegetables in it, to encourage fat loss. [6] [7]

6. **Eat fermented foods** - Foods like sauerkraut, kimchi and kombucha provide probiotics which improve gut health. Improved gut health can help with digestion and bioavailability of nutrients in other foods and improve immune function[8]. Try to get fermented foods into your diet daily or at least a few times a week.

7. **Use supplements correctly** - Supplements are not needed to be a good fighter. Training correctly, eating the right things and sleeping enough are far more important than taking supplements. With that said, supplements can aid in

performance and recovery, but like anything must be used correctly. The supplement industry is extremely unregulated, and lots of supplements end up having unlabeled performance enhancing drugs (PEDs) in them. Even trace amounts of PEDs, like prohormones, SARMs and various kinds of steroids can cause a fighter to fail a drugs test, potentially derailing their career. So the most important thing for a fighter or coach to know about supplements is that they are pure, containing what is listed and nothing else, through third-party testing. Even then, record what supplements are used and save the containers in case of a positive drug test. Assuming a supplement is what the label says, the next thing to consider is what supplements are worth taking. Some expensive supplements offer insignificant increases in performance or recovery that a fighter could multiply many times over simply by eating and sleeping better for a small fraction of the cost. Because of this, I only recommend these basic supplements to my fighters.

a. **High quality protein powder** - Protein is an essential macronutrient for the production of enzymes, hormones and many tissues in the body including muscle. For supplementation purposes a good choice is whey protein that is consumed post-workout or in place of a meal in a pinch. Casein protein is good before bed, as it is slower to digest and will sustain higher amino acid levels during the night.

Read the label on the protein container and find the serving size in grams, then subtract the amount of protein per serving in grams. The number left over is how many grams of "other stuff" is in the supplement. Find one with the least amount of "other stuff". Each serving should be about 30 to 40 grams of actual protein, which will help you reach the daily goal of .7 to 1 gram of protein per pound of bodyweight.

b. **Branched chain amino acids (BCAAs)** - These are three of the essential amino acids that make up a complete protein: leucine, isoleucine and valine. Lacking all the essential amino acids, BCAAs are not ideal as a stand-alone supplement for muscle recovery and growth. However, they are excellent to take before, during and after a workout to reduce fatigue, or during fasting periods to help preserve muscle. Leucine, one of the three BCAAs, plays a large role in the initiation of protein synthesis. This is why you should get a BCAA supplement that has the ratio 2:1:1 on it, meaning it contains two grams of leucine for every one gram of isoleucine and valine. Higher ratios are not necessarily better though. There is a ton of great research on BCAAs, and anecdotally I have found them to be very helpful with my fighters, especially while losing weight. Dosage should be between 2 to 10 grams at a time. Fair warning, the unflavored pure BCAAs I recommend to my fighters taste terrible, which usually ends up being the limiting factor in dosage.[9]

c. **Creatine** - Creatine provides a phosphate group to convert ADP to ATP, increasing the amount of time an athlete can rely on the phosphagen system, the bioenergetic system that fuels high intensity activities for bursts of around 10 seconds or less. This allows athletes to get one or two more reps in a heavy set while lifting, improving strength over time. Creatine also increases water retention, so it is important to cease use four weeks out from competition if a fighter is going to be cutting any weight. Creatine comes in different forms with different advantages and disadvantages. Personally I have used pure unflavored micronized creatine monohydrate for years. It is cheap and works, but feel free to try out other types. Dosage should be between 2 and 5 grams a day.[10]

d. **Magnesium** - Magnesium is a mineral that is essential for many of the body's functions and for maximum athletic performance. Athletes often require more magnesium than the average Joe, making supplementation even more important. Magnesium can help with sleep, so I recommend taking it at night. There is a lot of debate online as to what form of magnesium is best, so I prefer that my fighters get a supplement with multiple forms of magnesium such as gluconate, oxide, citrate and chloride, but at the end of the day any form of magnesium is better than none. Dosage should be between 300 and 500 milligrams a day.

e. **Vitamin D3 -** Vitamin D is essential for calcium and phosphorus regulation, bone density, muscle function and of course maximum performance. A shockingly high percentage of the US population is deficient, between 40% and 77% depending on what sources you trust. The easiest way to get vitamin D is to take your shirt off and go outside, but this is not always an option so supplementation may be necessary, particularly for athletes with darker skin, those living in the northern part of the US and Canada or during the winter months. Vitamin D is fat soluble, meaning it can accumulate in fat and toxicity is possible, so like most things, more is not always better. Ideally an athlete should have their vitamin D levels checked with a blood test and dose supplementation appropriately, but 1,000 to 2,000 IUs a day of D3 during the winter is generally accepted as a safe amount. [11]

f. **Omega 3s -** These are a type of polyunsaturated fat that have a ton of studies demonstrating their benefits including the lowering of inflammation, decreased anxiety, lower triglyceride levels and improved brain health after trauma, which is extremely important for fighters post-concussion. If a fighter has been knocked out or dropped badly, have them consume lots of DHA, a type of omega 3, for the next few weeks or even months. Ideally an athlete would get most of their omega 3s from food sources, such as fish, chia seeds and walnuts, but when that is not sufficient find a high-quality supplement. Lower quality and old supplements can turn rancid. Dosage around 3 grams, or 3,000 milligrams, a day seem to be safe and effective. Be sure to read supplement labels carefully though. Most omega 3 supplements are somewhere in the neighborhood of 1,000mg per serving, but only around 300mg of EPA and DHA, the actual omega 3s. In this case to get to 3,000mg of omega 3s, an athlete would need 10 servings throughout the day. If possible find a quality omega 3 supplement with higher potency to reduce the number of servings needed.[12][13][14][15]

g. **Turmeric** - Turmeric is a spice containing a chemical called curcumin, which has host of benefits including anti-aging, retention of cognitive functions and potential reductions in cancerous and precancerous cells. Be sure the turmeric supplement you use has black pepper extract or piperine, which greatly increases the bioavailability of the curcumin in the turmeric. Doses between 1,000mg and 2,000mg per day seem to be safe and effective. [16][17][18]

This is not a comprehensive list of supplements that can help a fighter, but rather a set of basic, effective and safe supplements that I recommend to my athletes and use myself. Personally, I love to read studies on substances that may improve cognitive function, athletic performance and overall health and longevity, and then experiment and try them out on myself. However, as a coach you cannot give your athletes anything unless you are 100% sure it is safe, effective and does not contain any banned substances.

— Chapter 10 —

Neck Strength

 Neck strength is absolutely essential in combat sports. Aside from the enhanced ability to transfer force and use your head as a tool while clinching and wrestling, a stronger neck helps a fighter avoid concussions. In fact, one study I found states that: "For every one pound increase in neck strength, odds of concussion decreased by 5%." [19] That is a significant number that makes chasing neck strength a worthwhile goal for any combat sports athlete.

 When I was boxing in college, the current push for understanding, treating and preventing concussions in combat sports was picking up and I was obsessed with strengthening my neck to avoid brain damage. I used all the classic boxing movements, hanging my head off the side of the ring while flexing, extending and rotating my neck in different patterns, working up to very high reps and even using a head weight while doing so. In addition, I used the four-way neck machine at the local gym whenever I would lift and hit bridges on the grappling mats or on an exercise ball. At this time I was also looking into physical therapy as a profession and always bugged the PTs I was around to show me neck exercises, that I would then force upon my boxing training partners. Despite all of this effort I only gained a small carryover to my perceived ability to take a punch and in the size of my neck.

The first time my neck really started to feel stronger in the ring was a complete accident. Some days I would wake up at six in the morning to run, go to class for a few hours, study and do homework in the afternoon, box from six to eight in the evening, sneak in a lift, then grab a sandwich on my way to teach the boxing club from nine till eleven. Obviously a drawn-out lifting program was out of the question, so my solution was to just do power hang cleans, which would later be a huge influence in my minimalist programming. My neck started to feel significantly stronger when I was sparring and even grew a bit. Now this is strictly anecdotal evidence showing that when a 21-year-old kid did a heavy compound lift his whole body, including the neck, grew. Not exactly groundbreaking news in the world of strength and conditioning. However, I believe the explosive nature of the clean creates a more specific training stimulus that carries over to absorbing a punch. The upper trap and surrounding musculature are forced to contract hard and quickly against a relatively high force. This is where the true value in cleans, snatches, high pulls and their variations lie in the context of combat sports. To apply this, simply program these movements into the power hinge section of your lifting cycle for athletes who are lacking in neck strength, being sure to cue the shrug motion at the top of the initial pull. However, neck training can go deeper than throwing some Olympic lifts into your fighter's program.

In November, 2015, I was given the opportunity to train at 13 Coins in Bangkok. At this point I had been training Muay Thai seriously for about a year, and had done a bit of clinch work, but nothing resembling the clinch training the Thais were doing and I had never seen neck strength like that before. Young fighters, maybe 12 years old, could pick each other up from within a full plum clinch position. Some of them, including Sangmanee, a multiple-time champion and fighter of the year, could even lift me off the floor with their necks when I tried to break their posture, despite my 40-plus pound weight advantage. The secret to their insane neck strength certainly did not lie in advanced weightlifting techniques; I never saw any type of formal structured strength training at all. Nor did it lie in freakishly thick necks due to genetics; most of the Thai fighters are thin and ectomorphic. However, they all clinch for at least half an hour during their daily training sessions, and once I took the time to break down the physiological training effect that must have had, it made total sense.

    When clinching, the neck undergoes flexion, extension, lateral flexion and rotation under a wide variety of loading parameters. More so than any other training modality or sport in my opinion. Sometimes the neck muscles are forced to contract explosively, when a training partner tries to break your posture or attempt a throw. Sometimes the neck muscles are contracted isometrically, to maintain posture or resist a face press defense. The load ranges from the weight of your training partner's arm in a light collar tie, all the way up to above their body weight when aggressively breaking posture. When performed for an extended period of time the neck muscles lift and resist a high total tonnage and are exposed to serious time under tension in a wide variety of directions.

After that first eye-opening training trip to Thailand, I clinched at every opportunity I had. Aside from improving my clinching abilities, my neck strength grew more than ever before, and I felt a carryover of that strength to my grappling and boxing training. So how can the benefits of clinching be incorporated into the overall strength and conditioning system? Simple, clinch as much as possible under the guidance of an experienced Muay Thai coach. When I run striking practices for our fight team, I generally leave 15 to 30 minutes at the end for live clinch training so my fighters cannot only dominate in the clinch, but also develop the extreme neck strength required for combat sports. Now if you do not have a knowledgeable Muay Thai coach or participate in a sport like western boxing, where there is no clinching, but neck strength is still required, a few Muay Thai drills can be incorporated into the programming. Two simple movements that will develop neck strength are the hip in posture retainment, and the face press defense, which are demonstrated below. These can be thrown in as ancillary movements, part of the warmup, or in skill practices, depending on what the athlete needs. While strength improvements can still be made with sub-par technique, these drills are best under the supervision of a good Muay Thai coach. Start conservatively with very little partner resistance and slowly progress to a higher intensity.

1. **Hip in posture retainment:**
    a. One athlete will start bent at the hips with their chest facing the floor and with a weak, flexed, protracted neck position.

    b. Before initiating any larger body movements, they will pack their neck by retracting and extending. Cue them to make a double chin and a big neck muscle.

    c. Maintaining the packed neck position, with resistance on the back of the head from a partner, walk the hips under the shoulders, until upright.

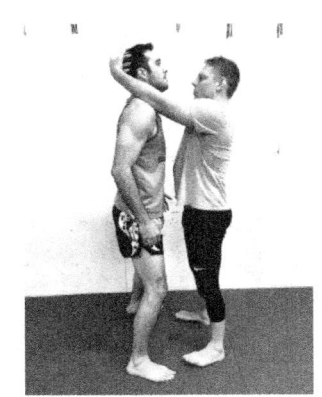

d. Start with very light partner resistance and gradually work up until you can lift your partner off the ground.

2. **Face press defense:**
   a. Start in a plum clinch position, with both hands high on the back of the head, elbows together against the chest, chin off to one side, upper body upright and a square stance. The partner being clinched must resist to maintain a tight, upright packed neck position.

   b. The fighter being clinched will reach outside and over to grab their partner's chin with both hands, using it as a handle to rotate the neck.

c. Once the neck is fully rotated, extend the arms until the clinch is broken.

d. The partner who started in the clinch will weave the arms underneath and inside, one at a time, to establish their own plum position.

e. Start again with the roles reversed. Both partners should keep their neck strong and resist an appropriate amount, slowly resisting more and more as their strength improves.

— Chapter 11 —

Tracking Sheets

"The faintest ink is more powerful than the strongest memory"
-Chinese proverb

An often overlooked, but vital part of a strength and conditioning system, is tracking training sessions. Quite frankly it barely matters exactly how workouts are tracked as long as they are. I like to make old school paper packets with a full cycle worth of training sessions on it that also includes the set and rep scheme on the last page. It is an easy format for the athletes to follow and write in the intensity and reps for each main exercise. It also makes things easier to change as a coach when one fighter needs to do something slightly different, due to an injury or a fight coming up. Simply substitute an exercise out or program different set and rep schemes depending on what the individual athlete needs. If you have a tracking app for your team or simply have athletes write their lifts in a notebook, that is fine as long as it works for you.

The example tracking sheet for a week shown below is how my team records our training sessions. I put two days' worth of workouts, or one week, on each side of the paper, making a full cycle a four-page, double-sided packet. This leaves enough space for fighters to put notes in the margins, which I highly encourage. The weight and body fat sections are extremely helpful once an athlete has built up a few months or years' worth of training. It allows you to see relative strength instead of just overall PRs and compare an upcoming weight cut with past performances. To complete and track the workout, an athlete simply starts in the top left corner, working and tracking left to right, row by row as if reading a page of text. Each cell with an "x" in it is meant for the athlete to record their intensity and reps. For example, if a fighter does a set of squats with 225lbs for four reps, the fighter would write "225 x 4". In the case of an unweighted box jump or other non-weighted exercise, the intensity would be the height of the box. A fighter who does a set of three box jumps on a high box would put "high box x 3" in that cell. Ancillary exercises simply have a check-off box next to them. This is to emphasize that most of those exercises are not meant to be overloaded to the same degree as the main lifts. You do not want an overzealous fighter grinding out heavy reps of dumbbell external shoulder rotations desperately trying to beat what they did last week.

Week 1

Date:	Weight:	BF%:
Power Snatch	x	☐ Dislocates
Set 2	x	☐ No Moneys
Set 3	x	☐ TRX Fallouts
Romanian Deadlift	x	☐ Scapular Pushup
Set 2	x	☐ Clamshells
Set 3	x	☐ Hang Stretch
DB Bench + Inverted Rows	x	x
Set 2	x	x
Set 3	x	x

Date:	Weight:	BF%:
Box Jump	x	☐ Hip Flexor Stretch
Set 2	x	☐ Hanging Side Crunch
Set 3	x	☐ Batwing 5x10 second
Front Squat	x	☐ Wall Angels
Set 2	x	☐ Hip Circles
Set 3	x	☐ Split Stretch
Handstand Pushup + Chins	x	x
Set 2	x	x
Set 3	x	x

While there are cells to record weight and body fat, you will notice there is no other tracking such as bar velocity, heart rate, etc. There are two main reasons for this. First of all the price of the technology is often not worth the value of the data collected. As a strength and conditioning coach I would love to have bar velocity trackers on every bar my athletes use and that data would hold some value. It would help me know when my athletes need to use more or less weight, if they are starting to overtrain, create friendly competition and be really cool, if nothing else. However, I can easily see when one of my athletes is going too slow on an Olympic lift and tell them to decrease the weight. Just by talking and paying attention to them I know when they have been training too much or not recovering enough as well. If my athletes were going to be competing in weightlifting, then that data would hold more value, but my fighters lift to be better fighters, not better lifters. The price of equipping all the bars in our weight room with velocity trackers would be high, while the value of the data gained would be small for my fighters.

The second reason most tracking technology is not worth it for our purposes, even if the technology is cheap, is the data collected often does not affect the decisions on how a fighter will train. For example, heart rate monitors are relatively inexpensive and easy to use, but a lot of the data that comes from them is of no use to a coach. If you are tracking heart rates during a fight sim four weeks out to see how fast after the workout a fighter's heart rate returns to normal, then compare that to the same measurement three weeks out, you would expect to see the recovery time decrease as the athlete gets into better shape and the movements become more efficient. Regardless of whether or not that time increased or decreased, that close to a fight I would still have the fighter finish out the remaining scheduled fight sims to continue building efficiency of movement in a fatigued state and increase mental toughness. I would also stress recovery to that athlete, regardless of the recorded recovery metrics because of how close they are to competition. Therefore, while the heart rate measurements may be cheap and easy to collect, they may not help a coach make more informed decisions about training and serve no purpose in this instance. Such measurements would only waste time, particularly when there are multiple athletes training or peaking out on the same schedule.

In the future as technology becomes cheaper, the ROI for certain measuring devices may increase to the point that using them makes sense. Also, if cost is not a limiting factor or you already have a measuring device, such as a HRV monitor, that you use to make informed decisions about your athlete's training, you should certainly use every resource at your disposal. I am not against using any particular type of tracking and you should not be either, just be sure that the measurements you take help you make better decisions for your athlete and know that fancy tracking devices are not a necessary part of an athlete's training protocol.

— Chapter 12 —

Application to Non-MMA Combat Sports

In the beginning of this manual I introduced the concept that some requirements of a fighter's strength and conditioning program are met through the sport of MMA itself. However, for combat sports that are not as inclusive as MMA, some minor changes will be made to the programing. For simplicity, non-MMA combat sports will be divided into striking-only sports, such as boxing and kickboxing, and grappling-only sports, such as jiu-jitsu and wrestling. However, a good strength and conditioning coach should be able to identify specific needs within their athletes' sport and personal anthropometry and adjust as necessary.

The training stimulus provided by practicing striking-only sports is great for explosivity but lacks in neck strength, isometric ab strength and grip strength, relative to full MMA training. The most important of those is neck strength. The three easiest ways to ensure a strong neck in this system is to first prioritize an Olympic lift, or variation of one, as the power hinge and give cues to emphasize the shrug at the top of the initial pull to strengthen the traps. Second, program a neck exercise or two as ancillaries, such as banded neck holds and bridges. Last, warm up or cool down with 5 to 10 mins of the two exercises outlined in the neck strength chapter. They can be done before or after skill practices as well for greater frequency.

Isometric ab strength and grip strength will definitely improve to some degree from basic lifts like overhead presses and deadlifts. However, for those who just feel they need the extra work or for a striker who is actually weak in those areas, simply program grip and isometric ab exercises, like a hanging L sit, as an ancillary or as an addition to the warmup or cooldown. For the hanging L sit specifically, when the athlete can no longer hold the L sit position, drop the legs down and just hang to burn out the grip as well as to get all the benefits from a hang stretch.

In contrast, the training stimulus provided by training grappling-only sports is excellent for strength and full-body tension development, but will generally lack in the attributes at the high speed end of the force-velocity curve and will often enforce bad posture. Grapplers should prioritize faster explosive exercises and ancillaries when possible to build speed. For example, use a banded overspeed jump over a weighted box jump or a rotational med ball throw over a Pallof press. Bar speed should be the top priority when performing Olympic lifts or explosive kettlebell exercises.

From a postural standpoint, a wrestling stance is a nightmare of spinal flexion with a protracted neck and shoulders. To combat this, program a lot of ancillary spinal mobility drills, like cat cows, shoulder retraction exercises, like band pull aparts, and variations of cervical retractions. Again, these can be used before or after skill practices as well for greater frequency.

These are just a few basic principles that broadly apply to striking and grappling sports, but the same thought process can go into any sport with more specificity. For example, a gi-only jiu-jitsu player may have serious stiffness and a lack of mobility in the hands and fingers, which could be combated with banded finger extensions and hand mobilities, programmed as ancillaries, warmups, or during a cooldown. What is really important is that as a coach or athlete you can pick out the performance or postural shortcomings within your specific sport, identify drills and exercises to balance out those shortcomings and program them correctly.

— Chapter 13 —

Mental Training

    I have always been intrigued by the mind and its power over the body's performance. In high school I read about seemingly mystical Shaolin monk training, watched Derren Brown exploit the weaknesses and patterns of human psychology and read everything I could about NLP and other sorts of applied psychology. Later in college, my interest continued in an excellent sport psychology class taught by Dr. Semyon Slobounov, whose principles I started to apply to my own boxing training. This was also the same time that GSP was the welterweight king and explained in interviews about how visualization helped him overcome fear and perform during fights, which I too tried to mimic. After graduating I slowly pieced together techniques and methods for mental training, which I distilled down into two basic phases and carried out with great success in April, 2015, during the season 22 TUF tryouts in Las Vegas with my top fighter, "Iron City" Mike Wilkins.

    Before breaking down the phases of mental training, a full disclosure: I am not a psychologist, and have simply applied some basic mental techniques to the fight game in a way that has worked for me and my athletes. What I will describe here is effective, but only the tip of the iceberg and for more in-depth or specific mental performance issues an athlete should see an actual sports psychologist.

    The first phase of mental training is to use meditation so a fighter can clear their mind and gain some conscious control over their thoughts, making them more receptive to the visualization in phase two. This meditation should ideally be done year-round, but starting a few weeks out from competition will still produce good results. For the TUF tryouts, Mike was fully on board with regular meditation a few weeks before we flew to Vegas. As with a strength training program, athlete buy-in and trust in the system is absolutely essential for mental training. During these weeks Mike and I would go to a quiet, comfortable place, sit or lie comfortably, set a timer for three to ten minutes and simply focus on breathing. With each inhalation the focus is on expanding the stomach and ribs horizontally and filling the lungs bottom up. Each exhalation is controlled and completely empties the lungs. As thoughts enter the mind do not fight against them, acknowledge them and visualize the thought drifting out of your head and return the focus to breathing. It may take some time or even a few meditation sessions, but eventually the fighter's mind will reach a state where the thoughts no longer pop up, there is extreme calm and the minutes fly by in what seems like seconds. The goal is to reduce the amount of time it takes to reach this state as the athlete gets closer to the second phase and competition. When Mike and I first started practicing meditation we would often not get to this state and anticipate the timer for the last few minutes. By the time we were packing for our flight, Mike had gained so much control over his mind that he could reach this state within two minutes and would be surprised when the timer went off "so quickly".

    The second phase is very specific visualization of the competition day. This should be done once or twice a day and start between the beginning of fight week to a few days before competition. First the athlete begins meditation as practiced before for a few minutes to clear the mind. Then, a coach describes the day of the event in as much detail as possible, mentioning specific techniques that were practiced and the inevitable feelings of anxiousness before a fight. The more senses that are engaged and specific details mentioned the better. Mike and I started somewhat vague visualizations a few days before leaving Pittsburgh, and gathered more information to improve the quality and detail of the visualizations as soon as we got to our hotel in Vegas. We walked from our room to the conference room that tryouts were held in and I took notes the whole way. I knew the exact route we would take, how many staircases and escalators we would use, where the pungent oyster bar we would pass was, the type of heavy glass door we would step through into the conference room and the faint patterns we would see on the wallpaper once we were inside. Twice on that first day we cleared the furniture in our room to the walls and went through our visualization before practicing the striking routine we had developed on mitts. After a few minutes of meditation, when I could tell Mike had cleared his mind, I would describe our walk to the conference room in great detail. I mentioned the lights and sounds from the slot machines in the casino, the smell of the oyster bar we passed, the emotions of excitement as we entered the conference room and saw all the competition. Using my understanding of Mike's elite jiu-jitsu game, I described how the grappling round would go. He would apply hard top pressure, pass guard and slap on his vicious guillotine. I described how the adrenaline would wear off, and we would move on to the striking round, where he would blend his boxing and wrestling, only communicating with the codes we had developed for each technique and combination weeks before we arrived. This way when he actually experienced the tryouts it would not feel like the first time. He would be a veteran of the process because he already "lived" the experience in his head many times over.

Unsurprisingly, the next day at tryouts Mike walked in with a champion's confidence and the day unfolded almost as we expected. The grappling round went eerily like we envisioned. Starting on the knees against a strong purple belt, Mike double legged (thighed?) his opponent, passed his guard, tapped him with a guillotine and was well on his way to repeating the process when the round ended. The striking round was sharp, and Mike clearly stood out as one of the more technical fighters. Unfortunately, in the final round, despite his elite skill and making it into the last group of 40 fighters down from the initial 411, the producers decided not to use him for the show. For better or worse, Mike is a genuinely good person, which does not always make for the most entertaining television.

Despite our initial disappointment, this trip ended up being one of the most valuable experiences for us as a fighter and coach. The mastery we had gained over visualization and the mental game was well worth the temporary pain.

Our technique is very simple in theory:

1. Meditate to gain control of the mind and allow it to be responsive to visualization.
2. Visualize in extreme detail all the physical steps, emotions and other senses the fighter will experience on competition day.

In practice it can be a bit more nuanced and a coach needs to know their fighter to be able to cater to their thought processes and mental state. A newer fighter may require hearing more detail about the process of being in a locker room and feeling the boredom and anxiety of waiting to fight, while an experienced pro may need to hear more about the techniques that make up their game plan for a specific opponent.

One last sport psychology 101 principle I would like to touch on, which is important for knowing how to deal with individual fighters in the hours and moments just before a fight, is the Yerkes-Dodson law, or the inverted U theory of arousal shown in the image below. Simply put, an athlete will perform best at a certain level of arousal, and performance will decrease with any more or less arousal. A fighter who is too calm may not be able to "turn it on" at the beginning of a fight, while a fighter who is too fired up may abandon technique and blow out their gas tank. Knowing your fighter's natural temperament and how they fight best is essential for how you will communicate with them before a fight and whether or not you need to get them amped up or to calm down. Some people are naturally calm and some excited. Some people fight best methodically and some recklessly. Know your fighter and do everything in your power to put them into the best mental state possible.

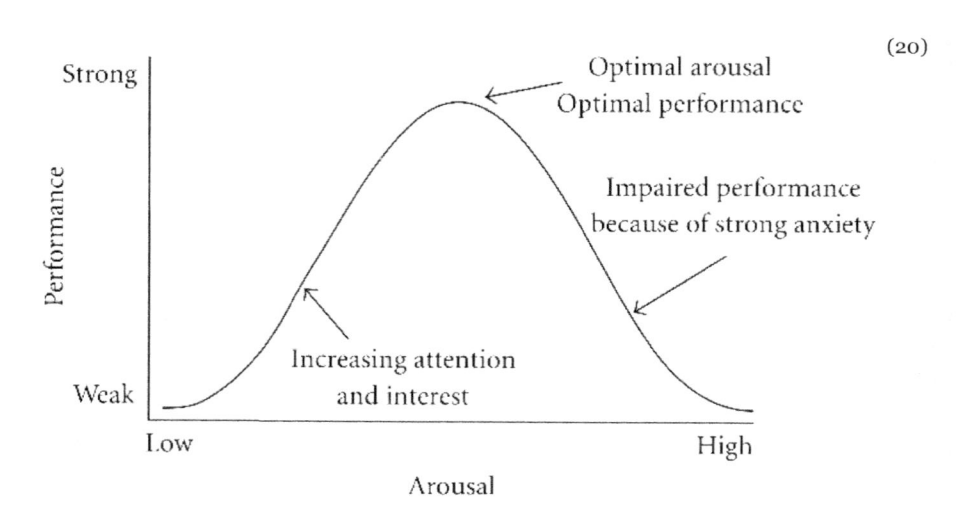

(20)

— Chapter 14 —

Movement Tables

The following tables are an incomplete list of exercises that will work within this system. There are plenty of movements and drills not listed that will be just as effective, especially in the ancillary category. There are whole books written on mobility, stability, flexibility, potentiation and breathing exercises, so please learn about them and use them with your fighters. These tables should be used as a reference when programing, not a way to learn an exercise. If you are unsure about how to perform any of these exercises, look for a video online or better yet get yourself a qualified coach.

Power Hinge

Single or Double KB Swing	Counts as an eccentric hamstring exercise
Single or Double KB Snatch	Be sure to hinge like a swing, not a squat
Uni or Bilateral Broad Jump	Great to use if superset with a strength hinge
Clean	Any variations are good, I prefer power cleans from a hang position for fighters
Snatch	Any variations are good
High Pull	Focus on bar speed, good regression for snatch and clean

Power Squat

Squat Jump	Great for beginners, maintain "knees out" position throughout movement
Box Jump	Takes force off the landing making it more joint friendly than a squat jump
Depth Drop	Best for more advanced lifters
Dumbbell Snatch	Focus on speed instead of just weight
Lunge Jump	Fixes power imbalances between legs

Strength Hinge

Deadlift	Drop from the top if you have bumper plates
Rack Pull	Allows for heavier loading
Trap Bar Deadlift	Good for athletes lacking full mobility
Snatch Grip Deadlift	Increases range of motion and improves grip strength
Romanian Deadlift (RDL)	Counts as an eccentric hamstring exercise
Good Morning	Counts as an eccentric hamstring exercise, do not get carried away with heavy loading
Barbell Hip Thrust	Google "Bret Contreras"

Strength Squat

Back Squat	Allows for heavy loading
Front Squat	Quad dominant, builds ab and upper back strength
Box Squat	A favorite of Westside, worth doing for that alone
Goblet Squat	Almost impossible to do wrong, great for beginners or as mobility exercise
Zercher Squat	Quad dominant, builds ab and upper back strength
Belt Squat	Great for athletes with spinal issues
Double KB Racked Squat	Builds serious ab strength with relatively light load
Pistol	Regression - hold on to rings Progression - hold on to dumbbells
Bulgarian Split Squat	Fixes strength imbalances, load with a barbell or dumbbells
Lunge	Fixes strength imbalances, use any variation such as walking, reverse and lateral

Upper Body Press

Barbell Overhead Press	Allows for heavy loading
Dumbbell Overhead Press	Fixes strength imbalances, builds stability
Single or Double KB Overhead Press	Forces proper movement, more joint-friendly
Barbell Incline Bench Press	Great way to change up pressing angle
Dumbbell Incline Bench Press	Fixes strength imbalances, builds stability
Landmine Press	Great way to change up pressing angle
Barbell Floor Press	Allows for extremely heavy loading
Barbell Bench Press	Allows for heavy loading with good range of motion
Single or Double Dumbbell Bench Press	Fixes strength imbalances, builds stability
Dip	Great way to change up pressing angle, Allows for heavy loading

Upper Body Pull

Pull or Chin-Up	Use all variations and grips. Regression - use bands for assistance or eccentric reps
Inverted Row	Easily scalable
Barbell Row	Allows for heavy loading, builds posterior chain
Pendlay Row	Forces stricter form
Chest Supported Row	Forces even stricter form
Dumbbell Row	Fixes strength imbalances

Gymnastic Press

Handstand Pushup	Regression - feet on box with hips flexed to 90°, or with feet against wall Progression - hands on blocks to increase range of motion
Single Arm Pushup	Regression - against wall, against bench, archer pushups Progression - elevate feet
Ring Pushup	Regression - pushup, iso hold in top position Progression - elevate feet, add resistance, ring fly
Ring Dip	Regression - dip on bar, iso hold in top position, use band for assistance
Planche Pushup	Regression - pushup with hands at hips, elevate feet, crow stand

Ancillary: Remember to emphasize movements from the first three tables

Scapular and Glenohumeral Control

Dislocates	Use bands or a PVC
Hang Stretch	Excellent for the shoulders and the spine
Facepull	Use bands, cables or a TRX, pull from all angles
Band Pull Apart	Keep the shoulders low and ribs down
No Moneys	Grab a band with a supinated grip, elbows stay at the sides, pull the band apart and retract the scapula
I, Y, T, W	Use a TRX, a band or light dumbbells while prone on a bench
Dumbbell External Rotations	Can be done seated with the elbow up on the knee, or in a side lying position
Bat Wings	Lie prone on a bench with dumbbells in the hands, pull the weights to the armpits and retract the scapula
Scapular Pushup	Builds strength in the serratus anterior
Scapular Pull-Up	Be sure to keep elbows straight
Wall Angels	Keep the hips, upper back, elbows and wrist against the wall
Prone PVC Behind the Neck Press	Narrow the grip to increase difficulty
PVC Bradford Press	Hold the head still, focus on scapular movement not arm movement
PVC Overhead Squat	Also great for increasing hip mobility
Kettlebell Armbar	Keep the arm locked and shoulder packed
Kettlebell Windmill	Excellent for hip and thoracic mobility as well
Kettlebell Bottoms-Up Press	Good patterning movement for overhead presses
Roll Shoulder Joint	Best with a LAX ball

Spinal Mobility and Traction

Hang Stretch	Excellent way to decompress the spine, pairs well with exercises that load the spine such as heavy squats
Manual Cervical Traction	Lie supine on a bench, a partner grips the mastoid process on each side and pulls the head away from the body, release tension slowly
Partner Extension Stretch	On both knees face a bench, put both elbows on the bench, partner presses down between scapula
Thoracic Rotation	Sit tall with hands on the side of the head, rotate to end range, crunch to the side and back up, rotate further and repeat three times per side
Cobra Stretch	Google "McKenzie Method" to truly appreciate this stretch
Yoga Bridge	Also great for shoulder mobility

Hip Mobility

Hip Circles	From a standing or quadruped position take the knee in a wide circle through a full range of motion, keeping the pelvis as still as possible, rotate both directions
Hip Flexor Stretch	Pairs well with squat movements, emphasize posterior pelvic tilt
Piriformis Stretch	Can be done supine or as a pigeon stretch
Split Stretch	Excellent for improving the quality and height of round kicks
Lateral Band Walk	Strengthens the glute medius and minimus and TFL, helps fix valgus knee issues
Clamshells	Strengthens the glute medius and minimus and TFL, helps fix valgus knee issues
Lateral Lunge	Keep the weight light when used as an ancillary exercise
Banded Hip Opener	Use any variety
LAX Ball/ Foam Roller	Dig in the hip flexors, piriformis, IT Band, etc.

Eccentric Hamstring

Nordic Hamstring Curl	Hold weight against the chest if necessary
GHD	Be sure the hips are free of the pad and you are not just doing spinal extensions
Roller Walk Out	Lay supine, with knees flexed place bottoms of feet on a foam roller, bridge onto shoulders, slowly walk the roller out then back in
Single Leg RDL	Focus on feeling the muscle instead of heavy loading

Abs/Core

Rollouts	Use an ab wheel, TRX, rings or a barbell, increase the weight on the bar to increase intensity
Janda Sit-Up	Wrap band around the ankles, flex knees to engage hamstrings against the band, crunch then sit up
L Sit	Use rings to increase intensity
Toes to Bar	Emphasize posterior pelvic tilt over hip flexion
Hardstyle Plank	Crunch "through" the floor
Pallof Press	Use bands or a cable
Wood Chops	Use bands or a cable
Landmine Rotations	Shove the end of a bar into a corner if you do not have a landmine
Windshield Wipers	Hang from a bar, bring feet up to the bar, rotate the pelvis till the legs are horizontal, then rotate to the other side
Rotational Med Ball Throw	Keep the weight fairly low and focus on speed
Hanging Side Crunch	Hang from a bar, crunch laterally, complete all reps on one side then the other

Specialty/Misc.

Breathing Drills	Use any variation, but most fighters just need the basic proper breathing mechanics, filling the lungs bottom up, expanding the bottom of the ribs 360°, in and out through the nose with slight spinal flexion.
Finger Extension	Use a finger band or bucket full of sand or rice
Pushup or Iso Hold on Knuckles, Back of Wrist and Fingertips	Slowly progress by shifting more bodyweight over the arms until you can hold a pushup position
Supination	Hold a hammer upside down, supinate the hand fully, hold for a second at the top, or use a band stretched across a power rack
Toe Curls	Sit with feet flat on the floor and a towel under the toes, curl the toes to grab the towel and pull it under the foot
Single Leg Balance	Stand on one foot, progress by closing eyes or standing on a yoga block, good for fighters regaining balance and proprioception after getting knocked out
Banded Neck Iso Holds	Wrap a band around the forehead, pack the neck, walk and hold, should be done at all angles

— Chapter 15 —

References

1. Verkhoshansky, Yuri, and Mel Cunningham. Siff. *Supertraining*. 6th ed., Verkhoshansky, 2009.
2. Monajati, A., Larumbe-Zabala, E., Goss-Sampson, M., & Naclerio, F. (2016). The Effectiveness of Injury Prevention Programs to Modify Risk Factors for Non-Contact Anterior Cruciate Ligament and Hamstring Injuries in Uninjured Team Sports Athletes: A Systematic Review. *Plos One, 11*(5). doi:10.1371/journal.pone.0155272
3. Cheung, K., Hume, P. A., & Maxwell, L. (2003). Delayed Onset Muscle Soreness. Sports Medicine, 33(2), 145-164. doi:10.2165/00007256-200333020-00005
4. Schoenfeld, B. J. (2010). The Mechanisms of Muscle Hypertrophy and Their Application to Resistance Training. *Journal of Strength and Conditioning Research, 24*(10), 2857-2872. doi:10.1519/jsc.0b013e3181e840f3
5. Chu, D. A., & Myer, G. D. (2013). *Plyometrics*; Champaign, Ill: Human Kinetics.
6. Jeukendrup, A. (2003). Modulation of carbohydrate and fat utilization by diet, exercise and environment. *Biochemical Society Transactions,31*(6), 1270-1273. doi:10.1042/bst0311270

7. Thompson, D. L., Townsend, K. M., Boughey, R., Patterson, K., & Jr, D. R. (1998). Substrate use during and following moderate- and low-intensity exercise: Implications for weight control. *European Journal of Applied Physiology, 78*(1), 43-49. doi:10.1007/s004210050385
8. Parvez, S., Malik, K., Kang, S. A., & Kim, H. (2006). Probiotics and their fermented food products are beneficial for health. *Journal of Applied Microbiology,100*(6), 1171-1185. doi:10.1111/j.1365-2672.2006.02963.x
9. Shimomura, Y., Murakami, T., Nakai, N., Nagasaki, M., & Harris, R. A. (2004). Exercise Promotes BCAA Catabolism: Effects of BCAA Supplementation on Skeletal Muscle during Exercise. *The Journal of Nutrition,134*(6). doi:10.1093/jn/134.6.1583s
10. Volek, J. S., Duncan, N. D., Mazzetti, S. A., Staron, R. S., Putukian, M., Gomez, A. L., Kraemer, W. J. (1999). Performance and muscle fiber adaptations to creatine supplementation and heavy resistance training. *Medicine & Science in Sports & Exercise,31*(8), 1147-1156. doi:10.1097/00005768-199908000-00011
11. Holick, M. F., & Chen, T. C. (2008). Vitamin D deficiency: A worldwide problem with health consequences. *The American Journal of Clinical Nutrition,87*(4). doi:10.1093/ajcn/87.4.1080s

12. Kiecolt-Glaser, J. K., Belury, M. A., Andridge, R., Malarkey, W. B., & Glaser, R. (2011). Omega-3 supplementation lowers inflammation and anxiety in medical students: A randomized controlled trial. *Brain, Behavior, and Immunity, 25*(8), 1725-1734. doi:10.1016/j.bbi.2011.07.229
13. Simopoulos, A. P. (2002). Omega-3 Fatty Acids in Inflammation and Autoimmune Diseases. *Journal of the American College of Nutrition, 21*(6), 495-505. doi:10.1080/07315724.2002.10719248
14. Goodfellow, J., Bellamy, M. F., Ramsey, M. W., Jones, C. J., & Lewis, M. J. (2000). Dietary supplementation with marine omega-3 fatty acids improve systemic large artery endothelial function in subjects with hypercholesterolemia. *Journal of the American College of Cardiology, 35*(2), 265-270. doi:10.1016/s0735-1097(99)00548-3
15. Lewis, M. D., & Bailes, J. (2011). Neuroprotection for the Warrior: Dietary Supplementation With Omega-3 Fatty Acids. *Military Medicine,176*(10), 1120-1127. doi:10.7205/milmed-d-10-00466
16. Rainey-Smith, S. R., Brown, B. M., Sohrabi, H. R., Shah, T., Goozee, K. G., Gupta, V. B., & Martins, R. N. (2016). Curcumin and cognition: A randomised, placebo-controlled, double-blind study of community-dwelling older adults. *British Journal of Nutrition,115*(12), 2106-2113. doi:10.1017/s0007114516001203

17. Cruz–Correa, M., Shoskes, D. A., Sanchez, P., Zhao, R., Hylind, L. M., Wexner, S. D., & Giardiello, F. M. (2006). Combination Treatment With Curcumin and Quercetin of Adenomas in Familial Adenomatous Polyposis. *Clinical Gastroenterology and Hepatology,4*(8), 1035-1038. doi:10.1016/j.cgh.2006.03.020
18. Shoba, G., Joy, D., Joseph, T., Majeed, M., Rajendran, R., & Srinivas, P. (1998). Influence of Piperine on the Pharmacokinetics of Curcumin in Animals and Human Volunteers. *Planta Medica,64*(04), 353-356. doi:10.1055/s-2006-957450
19. Collins, C. L., Fletcher, E. N., Fields, S. K., Kluchurosky, L., Rohrkemper, M. K., Comstock, R. D., & Cantu, R. C. (2014). Neck Strength: A Protective Factor Reducing Risk for Concussion in High School Sports. *The Journal of Primary Prevention, 35*(5), 309-319. doi:10.1007/s10935-014-0355-2
20. Diamond, D. M., Campbell, A. M., Park, C. R., Halonen, J., & Zoladz, P. R. (2007). The Temporal Dynamics Model of Emotional Memory Processing: A Synthesis on the Neurobiological Basis of Stress-Induced Amnesia, Flashbulb and Traumatic Memories, and the Yerkes-Dodson Law. *Neural Plasticity,2007*, 1-33. doi:10.1155/2007/60803

Printed in Great Britain
by Amazon